WISDOM
FOR THE
END TIMES

Colombia para Cristo video introduction

Watch the La Montaña trailer, a film based on a true Stendal event

WISDOM
FOR THE
END TIMES

FROM THE BOOK OF PROVERBS

A COMMENTARY

RUSSELL M. STENDAL

Visit Russell's website: www.cpcsociety.ca

Wisdom for the End Times – Russell M. Stendal

Copyright © 2016

First edition published 2016

Scripture quotations are taken from the Jubilee Bible (or Biblia del Jubileo), copyright © 2000, 2001, 2010, 2013 by Life Sentence Publishing, Inc. Used by permission of Life Sentence Publishing, Inc., Abbotsford, Wisconsin. All rights reserved.

Cover Design: Natalia Hawthorne (BookCoverLabs.com)
eBook Icon: Icons Vector/Shutterstock
Editors: Bronwen Jorel and Sheila Wilkinson

Printed in the United States of America

Aneko Press – *Our Readers Matter*[TM]

www.anekopress.com

Aneko Press, Life Sentence Publishing, and our logos are trademarks of Life Sentence Publishing, Inc.
203 E. Birch Street
P.O. Box 652
Abbotsford, WI 54405

RELIGION / Biblical Commentary / Old Testament

Paperback ISBN: 978-1-62245-320-7

eBook ISBN: 978-1-62245-341-2

10 9 8 7 6 5 4 3 2 1

Available where books are sold

Share this book on Facebook:

Contents

Introduction

A very important thing to understand in Proverbs (or in any other book of the Bible) is that God uses words according to his own meaning.

As the years and centuries and millennia pass, mankind causes not only ecological damage to the planet and corruption to society but perversion to language. A word that began with a certain meaning may no longer retain it; secondary meanings abound and, with the passage of time, may even tend to dominate. It often requires quite a bit of study to discover the depths of pure language that God promises to restore (Zephaniah 3:9).

When reading the book of Proverbs, it's extremely important to understand exactly what God means with each word. The Jubilee Bible translation uses, as much as possible within the limits of the English language, a unique English word for each unique and corresponding Hebrew word (based on the work of early Reformation scholars such as Casiodoro de Reina and William Tyndale). This eliminates, as far as possible, the use of synonyms (approximate equivalents of the original word) and mistranslation; in this way the Scripture defines itself more clearly for us through the usage that God gives to each word or phrase. The Jubilee Bible sheds an incredible amount of light upon the book of Proverbs that helps bring prophetic details into sharp focus.

Note that the book of Proverbs has to do with acquiring the understanding and wisdom to interpret parables and the words and enigmas of the wise (Proverbs 1:6). To do this, it uses contrast as a method of making its point on multiple levels. For example:

The fool is contrasted with the wise person. This is the first place in the Bible that this particular word for "fool" is introduced. It comes from an obscure root word meaning "to be perverse." The fool refuses to receive correction even though it would be to his benefit.

The wise, faithful woman is contrasted with another type of woman who is the path to death and perdition.

Good friendships are contrasted with evil ones.

There is a smooth way that seems right to the natural man, but in reality this is the road to perdition. There's another way where it seems that we'll lose not only the things of this world – things that we worked hard for and valued – but possibly even our own life. This way is uphill and against all odds. Yet this is the way to life. This is the way to the blessing. This is wisdom.

Chapter 1

The Chastening of Prudence

Proverbs 1

1 The Proverbs of Solomon, the son of David, King of Israel;

2 to know wisdom and chastening; to understand prudent words;

3 to receive the chastening of prudence, justice, judgment, and equity;

4 to give prudence to the simple, and to the young men knowledge and council.

Council is used here in the (old and now obsolete) sense that it is the ability to make determinations and decisions that will stand the test of time. The Hebrew word is distinct from the word translated as "counsel" in verse 5.

5 If the wise will hear them, doctrine shall increase, and the man of understanding shall acquire wise counsel:

6 *To understand a parable and the interpretation; the words of the wise and their enigmas.*

Many people cite a proverb here or a proverb there, according to convenience, but the book of Proverbs has a general sequence and structure, and within this book key words (terminology defined by their God-ordained usage in Scripture) are very important not only here but also throughout the rest of the Bible. This structure and vocabulary relates to the daily life of each and every one of us.

Consider, for example, the Lord's Prayer. When Jesus taught his disciples to pray, he included a reference to *our daily bread* (Matthew 6:11). This can be understood in the context that we *shall not live by bread alone, but by every word that proceeds out of the mouth of God* (Deuteronomy 8:3; Matthew 4:4).

In order to be properly nourished and sustained so we're able to adequately respond to whatever daily situations we may face, we need to be taking in food not just for our bodies but for our souls. Just as we can't expect to have healthy bodies if we fast for six days a week and then feast on the seventh, we cannot expect spiritual health unless we hear the voice of God on a continual basis rather than just one day a week.

Jesus told us not to worry about tomorrow (Matthew 6:34). We can't prepare in advance for every conceivable contingency that the morrow may bring; rather, we must seek wisdom from God to face each day that we live. Wisdom, however, is closely linked to a concept that we generally find much less desirable – chastening.

> 2 *to know wisdom and chastening; to*
> *understand prudent words;*
>
> 3 *to receive the chastening of prudence,*
> *justice, judgment, and equity;*

We tend to think that things like chastening and judgment are very negative, but they're actually helpful. Chastening has to do with discipline, with correction, and it's not possible for us to learn anything without it. For instance, if we try to teach mathematics and don't correct the students when they come up with a wrong answer, they'll never learn how to find the right one – how can they, when they don't know that their first answer is wrong?

Similarly, if God doesn't correct us (and that's what chastening is), then it will be impossible for us to really learn anything. The root word of *chasten* is *chaste*, which doesn't necessarily have a sexual connotation. It used to refer to having boundaries or limits that must be adhered to. In modern usage, to be chaste is to be sexually pure (abstinent prior to marriage and faithful thereafter), but the original meaning covers all areas of behavior. And because we're imperfect people, we cannot be chaste unless we're chastened from time to time.

In order for us to know wisdom, the Lord must place us and keep us within certain boundaries and certain ways of doing things. This is essential if we are to have understanding. It's not enough just to have the right goals; we must go about achieving them in the right way, his way. In the highest sense, Jesus is the way, the truth, and the life (John 14:6).

The Lord isn't satisfied in having a bunch of slaves who blindly follow him but don't understand anything. God desires for us to have wisdom and understanding so we, in turn, can be understood by others and by God. It's not possible to understand God's heart and God's ways unless we draw near to him, and it's not possible to remain near to him unless we receive his discipline and chastening upon our lives. God chastens his children whom he loves – indeed, he chastens us because he loves us – and the mature sons (and daughters) of God are the ones who are the heirs to his promises.

Sooner or later, all of us will be subject to the judgment of God. If we seek him early, of our own free will, then we will receive the *chastening of prudence* so we may be corrected now, before it's too late. This way, Father God will be able to shape and form us according to his good will. If we offer ourselves to him for his correction and allow him to remove from our hearts everything that he does not like, we will find ourselves bearing the good fruit of righteousness that he delights in.

Yielding ourselves wholly to the Lord is the only way that we can be balanced and walk in justice (the Hebrew word for this can also be translated as "righteousness"), judgment, and equity. Otherwise, the endeavors of men will always bounce back and forth between two extremes, such as legalism and licentiousness.

4 *to give prudence to the simple,*

The serpent represents the Devil several times in Scripture, which also mentions the prudence of the serpent. If the sons of the Devil are prudent as they vie for the power and things of this world, it might seem that many among the people of God lack this important trait. What is prudence? And why does God desire to give it to the *simple*?

The serpent and the sons of the Devil are prudent in the sense that they attempt to protect their own lives and do not take unnecessary risk. Prudence has to do with being practical and using common sense.

Voltaire tells us wryly that common sense is not so common, and it's hard to disagree with him on this score. That's because the common sense that he was referring to (like every other form of wisdom) comes from God, and most people refuse to be taught and corrected by him. Common sense is also linked to the conscience, which God has placed inside each one of us to prompt us to do things the world doesn't regard as common sense at all – even to the point of risking our lives according to the will of God.

The sons of this age seek the things of this world, most often power and possessions, and they're prudent in the sense that they know how to protect their own lives and how to guard the worldly things they've acquired. But the sons of the light often lack prudence, in that many times they're careless with their spiritual lives and their eternal inheritance because they complicate simple truth and mix the things of God with the ways of the world.

Let's look at that verse again.

> 4 *to give prudence to the simple, and to*
> *the young men knowledge and council.*

The simple are those who are sincere but naïve. They need prudence to stay on the path that is straight and narrow; they need prudence so they don't mix the ways and goals of God with the ways and values of the world; they need prudence in order to keep their eyes on the Lord instead of blindly submitting to those who claim to be their elders. The young men and women in God will then receive personal, firsthand knowledge of God and council; they will receive authority from God to make determinations that will stand the test of time.

> 5 *If the wise will hear them, doctrine shall increase,*

If the wise will hear whom?

The simple (sincere but naïve) and the young people who have set a simple course to line up with the will of God and have not allowed their lives to become complicated and mixed up – these are the ones who will be able to make decisions once they have prudence and personal knowledge of God. Those who are wise will hear them.

What is the doctrine that is to increase?

In many churches, the doctrines are the precepts that have been put in place by the human founders of the church or by those whom the church considers to be wise. These precepts are considered unalterable dogmas that must be learned, memorized, and adhered to by all of the adepts of that particular church or religion. Anyone who, in good conscience, no longer believes their doctrine will be considered a heretic and banished. In past centuries, passions about such dogma ran so high at times that many were killed over even slight doctrinal differences.

> 5 *If the wise will hear them, doctrine shall increase, and the man of understanding shall acquire wise counsel:*

Here doctrine is to be expanded on an individual basis to and through those who come under the direct dealings of God. Doctrine shall increase as God applies truth and discipline directly on a personal basis to each of his sons and daughters.

Without direct, personal, and continual contact with God, man will always go to extremes in a zigzag pattern from one error to another. Each time he perceives that he has been in error, he will overcorrect his course and head for the opposite error. Over time, the distance between his errors will grow greater and greater, and he will find himself ricocheting from one extreme to the other. We see this in every entity or situation under the control of man. Many countries, and even entire regions of the world, are divided in their opinions on a variety of subjects but chiefly religion and politics. These divisions grow over time and always produce misunderstanding, hardship, and loss of life. The Devil is expert at stirring up division and strife.

God, on the other hand, desires for us to be wise and for his doctrine to increase as he deals with us, so that we may be men and women of understanding who are able to identify and learn from (acquire) wise counsel. The original wording also implies that when this happens, we will be understood not only by God but also by others.

6 *To understand a parable and the inter-*
pretation; the words of the wise and their
enigmas.

Enigmas have to do with things that are certain but hidden, things that require wisdom if we are to understand them.

When the Lord Jesus came and taught the multitudes, his teaching methods often involved using parables or enigmas that require wisdom and understanding in order for the underlying truth to be perceived (Matthew 13:34-35). Those who held tight to the religion of men did realize that Jesus' parables were stories told against them, but their minds were so closed that they couldn't really understand the hidden truths he was conveying.

7 *The fear of the LORD is the beginning of*
knowledge, but fools despise wisdom and
chastening.

The beginning of knowledge is the beginning of firsthand experience with God. Knowledge in this sense comes before wisdom. To fear the Lord is not to cower before him; we're his children, and he's a loving Father. Rather, fearing the Lord means looking up to him and honoring him and respecting him above all else. This attitude is the beginning of knowledge, the beginning of coming to know him.

If we don't know God, we really don't know anything. Without him, what we think we know isn't wisdom. According to God, those who have the wisdom of this world without knowing him are actually fools.

8 *My son, hearken unto the chastening of*

*thy father, and forsake not the law of thy
mother:*

The Lord had to put the people of God under law
before it would be possible for them to have a direct
relationship with the Father. Under the Jewish system,
a child was under the law of their mother until age
twelve. Then they had to make a decision at a ceremony
called a bar mitzvah for boys, a bat mitzvah for girls.
The child had to decide and make his own declaration
that he or she was willing to submit to the authority
and chastening of the father. A young person was not
considered mature until the age of thirty; sons were
unable to receive an inheritance or enter into ministry
before that point. The Lord Jesus began his ministry at
about thirty years of age. Under Jewish law there were
big differences between the treatment of boys and girls.
In Christ, however, there is no male nor female and we
are all sons of God (Galatians 3:26-28).

To hearken means to hear and obey. Many religious
people mistakenly think that chastening is something
that they can unilaterally do to their children with a
rod. This isn't necessarily the case, because the chastening or correction of the father must be *hearkened unto.*
At the same time, the law of the mother, the precepts
by which she raised the child, must not be forsaken.
The curved end of the shepherd's rod (or crook) was
primarily for restraining the sheep that needed individual care from the shepherd. The straight end was
for beating off attacks by wolves or other predators and
was only used on the sheep in time of dire necessity.

The son is to submit to the voice of the father. Our true father is God, and none of us who have children will be successful parents unless our children recognize the authority of God and submit to him. We have a responsibility, not just to our children but also to God, to use our parental authority with wisdom, because if our children see a wrong or twisted concept of authority in us, their concept of God will be wrong and twisted. People who are hard on their children with a bad temper or out of their own demanding criteria will almost always lose them, because that type of parenting will produce resentment that can fester for years and then burst into open rebellion as soon as the children are old enough to be on their own.

> 8 *My son, hearken unto the chastening of thy father, and forsake not the law of thy mother:*
>
> 9 *For they shall be an increase of grace unto thy head and protection about thy neck.*

An increase of grace. What is the grace of God?

It can be defined in many ways. One way of seeing it is that the grace of God is the power of God to do for us that which we are unable to do for ourselves. From another perspective, the grace of God is the love of God to change and transform us. We must understand that God does not love the old man, that creature whose sinful human nature continually has rebellious wrong desires. God's plan is to destroy the old man even while he saves and restores our soul in the new man in Christ. This mighty work can only be accomplished by the grace of God.

Notice that the grace of God may increase upon us if we are careful with certain things. We can't transform our hearts and our minds on our own; we can't remove from our lives, all by ourselves, those things that the Lord doesn't like: God must intervene. And if we don't embrace the chastening of our heavenly Father and keep a clear vision of the law of our mother, there is no guarantee that the grace of God will increase upon us.

In the New Testament, the apostle Paul repeatedly writes that it's possible for the grace of God to be multiplied upon us. It can be a never-ending geometric progression of goodness and blessing. In the words of 1 Corinthians 2:9, *But as it is written, That which eye has not seen nor ear heard neither has entered into the heart of man is that which God has prepared for those that love him.* This is the plan that God has for each one of us, but it's something that's almost impossible for us to comprehend.

The proof that we love God is our willingness to receive his correction and guidance so he will grant us the grace to do his will.

> 10 *My son, if sinners entice thee, do not consent.*

Some of the sinners that entice Christians may even be masquerading as bona fide Christian leaders. Such leaders embrace a false gospel in which there is no victory over sin, over the world, or over the Devil. Their easy gospel promises carnal security and the prosperity of the things of this world, instead of the character of Christ and the fruit of the Spirit.

Why are so many people being deceived? Consider the words of Paul in 2 Thessalonians 2:10: *and with all deception of iniquity working in those that perish because they did not receive the charity of the truth, to be saved.*

The Devil may use any of his instruments, any of his intermediaries, to attack us. However, he will only cause us lasting damage if we make the wrong choices: that is, if we make decisions and determinations based on fear or on personal benefit instead of placing our life under the authority of God. Despite having the power of life and death over us, the Lord will not force us to make the right choices. If we don't willingly submit to his discipline, he will not correct and chasten us in the sense of making us chaste, as he desires – that we may hear and follow his voice. If we refuse to hear the right voice, we open the door to wrong voices, the voices of other spirits, voices that seek only to deceive us. As long as we willfully continue to make the wrong choices, perverse persons and situations that seem very smooth and harmless at first will entangle us more and more.

Returning to the words of Proverbs 1:

> 11 *If they say, Come with us, let us lay in wait for blood; let us ambush the innocent without cause.*

> 12 *Let us swallow them up alive as Sheol and whole as those that go down into the pit.*

Satan's problem from the very beginning was pride. It wasn't enough for him to have all of the wonderful gifts, capacities, and power that God granted him in the beginning when he was created. No, that wasn't sufficient to satisfy Satan's overweening pride. Instead, in an attempt to place himself above the throne of God, he *ambushed the innocent* Adam and Eve. Scripture refers to the foundation of the world (Luke 11:50) – a different matter from the creation of the heavens and the earth effected by God as described in Genesis.

Obviously, Satan usurped many things at the time of the fall, and since that time he has been known as the prince of this world due to his hold on lost humanity. In the New Testament the phrase "this world" refers primarily to the kingdom of Satan, which is a way of doing things as opposed to "the earth," which was created by God and still belongs to God, even though it is under the curse and awaiting redemption.

Worldly pride, however, is a spiritual danger. As the apostle James wrote: *know ye not that the friendship of the world is enmity with God? Whosoever therefore that desires to be a friend of the world, makes himself the enemy of God* (James 4:4). As always, Jesus points us to the path we are to follow: *Blessed are the meek* [those who submit to God] *for they shall inherit the earth* (Matthew 5:5, author's comment).

> 13 *We shall find all kinds of riches, we shall fill our houses with spoil.*
>
> 14 *Cast in thy lot among us; let us all have one purse.*

The Devil thought that he had spoiled God's entire creation here upon the earth. Scripture even grants him the title of "the god of this world." He invented the world system that is based on lies that lead to death, based on deception, and based on killing innocent persons and taking the spoil. He wants to get as many as possible to throw their lot in with him and consciously join him. He wants to get everyone to pursue the wrong goals and procure things the wrong way. If he can achieve that, he will control us. He wants to manage the purse, because he knows that where our money is, our heart is also (Matthew 6:21; Luke 12:34). It's interesting to note that Judas Iscariot managed the purse and dipped into it from time to time for personal gain. Contrast that with the behavior of the early Christians after the coming of the Holy Spirit: *And of the multitude of those that had believed was one heart and one soul; no one said that anything he possessed was his own, but they had all things common* (Acts 4:32).

Those early believers all had the heart and soul of Jesus, because his plan is to join all who are his into one body, the body of Christ. If one member of the body suffers, all suffer, and if one member of the body is exalted, all share in the success. This attitude wasn't the result of external teaching or of submission to human control; it was the result of the overflowing presence of the Holy Spirit in the early believers.

> 15 *My son, do not walk in the way with them; refrain thy foot from their path:*

This is wisdom speaking to all the sons of God.

> 16 *For their feet shall run to evil and make haste to shed blood.*

17 *Surely in vain the net is spread in the
sight of any bird.*

The bird will not allow itself to be caught if it can
see the net. Those who belong to Satan are spreading
a net to snare all of humanity, and those who are not
right with God can't see it.

18 *And they lay in wait for their own
blood; they ambush their own souls.*

What did the Devil do? He decided to ambush
Adam and Eve and take them out so he could take
over the creation that God had placed in their hands.
At first he seemed so successful that he was joined in
his rebellion by a third of the heavenly hosts. It wasn't
until thousands of years later, with the advent of Jesus
Christ, that it started to become more and more appar-
ent that the Devil and all of his followers have really
been lying in wait for their own blood. They have
ambushed their own souls. But Satan doesn't give up
easily, and he continues to seek fellow travelers who
are susceptible to his lures.

19 *So are the ways of every one that is
greedy of gain which takes away the life of
those who possess it.*

Many religious persons are *greedy of gain* in that
they use the gifts and ministries of God for personal or
corporate gain, not realizing that they have fallen into a
snare that will cost them their lives if they don't repent.
God is no respecter of persons. He's not impressed by
your Nielsen ratings; he doesn't care how many people

purchase your books or your CDs and DVDs. Everyone who is greedy of gain is on the path to perdition.

> 20 *Wisdom cries without; she utters her voice in the streets:*
>
> 21 *She cries in the chief place of concourse, in the entrance to the gates of the city she utters her words, saying,*
>
> 22 *How long, ye simple ones, will ye love simplicity? and the scorners delight in their scorning, and the fools hate knowledge?*

Notice that God defines knowledge a bit differently from the way it's defined at the universities of men.

> 23 *Return at my reproof; behold, I will pour out my spirit unto you, I will make known my words unto you.*

Here is the introduction of another key word: *reproof.* Reproof is when God tells us that he doesn't approve of what we're doing and how we're going about it. In this verse, a thousand years prior to the day of Pentecost, we have the promise of the pouring out of the Holy Spirit. In order for us to return, we must make a course reversal of 180 degrees; then he will pour out his Spirit upon us and cause us to know his words.

What will this pouring out of the Holy Spirit involve? Jesus said that when the Comforter (the Holy Spirit) is come, he will reprove the world of sin, of judgment, and of righteousness (John 16:8).

What will happen when we know God's words? Paul

wrote that *all scripture is given by inspiration of God and is profitable for doctrine, for reproof, for correction, for instruction in righteousness* (2 Timothy 3:16). If we have no direct dealings with the Lord, we cannot know him or have knowledge of his realm. It doesn't matter how intelligent or wise or gifted we think we are or how many letters we have after our name. True wisdom is only revealed by God, and he only reveals it to those that he knows. But we must accept that if we are to truly know him and become his friends, it's necessary for him to be able to correct or chasten us as needed.

When he pours out his Spirit upon us, we can know when his Spirit is sad and unhappy with what we're doing or not doing or with the way we're going about things. If we consent to his dealing with us, then revelation of the truth, his words, will spontaneously flow. If we don't consent, however, we may find ourselves numbered among the many religious people who really don't know God. Even though such people participate in daily or weekly religious exercises, they have never personally heard the voice of God. They are likely to have been thoroughly indoctrinated as adepts of a certain brand of religion. They may even be under the ministry of a pastor or priest or rabbi who does hear from God, but nevertheless they live sad, defeated lives because they're not under the personal discipline, correction, and chastening of Father God.

> 24 *Because I have called and ye refused; I have stretched out my hand, and no one responded;*

25 *for because ye have disregarded all my counsel and rejected my reproof:*

This rejection of God's discipline was the cause of Adam and Eve being banished from the garden of God; and to this day, it's the natural inclination of all of their descendants.

26 *I also will laugh at your calamity; I will mock when your fear comes upon you;*

27 *when what you have feared comes as destruction, and your calamity comes as a whirlwind; when tribulation and anguish come upon you.*

Great tribulation and anguish are prophesied upon Israel and the church at the end of the age, which is even now upon us (Daniel 12:1; Revelation 2:22-23). The time of Jacob's trouble is near. Some will be hidden and protected by the Lord and some will not (Psalm 91).

28 *Then they shall call upon me, but I will not answer; they shall seek me early, but they shall not find me:*

29 *Because they hated knowledge and did not choose the fear of the LORD:*

30 *They rejected my counsel: they despised all my reproof.*

There is a time when we may seek the Lord so that he may correct us, discipline us, and chasten us. If this time slips away, we have no guarantee that we will be able to return to him at a time of our own choosing.

In every generation, some people can only learn the hard way.

> 31 *Therefore they shall eat of the fruit of their own way, and be filled with their own counsel.*
>
> 32 *For the rest of the ignorant shall slay them, and the prosperity of fools shall destroy them.*
>
> 33 *But whosoever hearkens unto me shall dwell safely and shall rest from the fear of evil.*

Let Us Pray:

Lord, we ask that you may adjust our conceptions and our understanding of these words until we are lined up with you. We desire to submit to your discipline, correction, and chastening until even our dreams and the imaginations of our hearts are under your control. Amen.

Chapter 2

The Lord Gives Wisdom

Proverbs 2

1 My son, if thou wilt receive my words and hide my commandments within thee

2 so that thou incline thy ear unto wisdom and apply thine heart to intelligence,

3 yea, if thou criest for understanding and givest thy voice unto intelligence,

4 if thou seekest her as silver and searchest for her as for hid treasures,

5 then shalt thou understand the fear of the LORD and find the knowledge of God.

Here wisdom is personified. We may listen as she speaks and instructs us, but intelligence isn't a fixed mental quotient; rather, it is linked to the status of our heart. We may cry out for understanding and then lend or yield our voice to an intelligence vastly superior to our own.

This is the path towards understanding the fear of the Lord. This is the path to personal knowledge of Father God. Today, many claim to know Jesus; yet if their faith is superficial, if they do not have a proper understanding of the fear of the Lord, they won't come to know God the Father personally. And it's not possible to know the truth without knowing God. In the well-known words of 1 Corinthians 13:12, *For now we see as through a mirror, in darkness, but then we shall see face to face; now I know in part, but then I shall know even as I also am known.* Paul painted a similar word picture in 2 Corinthians 3:18 when he wrote, *Therefore we all, beholding as in a glass the glory of the Lord with uncovered face, are transformed from glory to glory into the same likeness, even as by the Spirit of the Lord.*

Without true knowledge of God, it's impossible to know anything of eternal importance. Without knowing God, it's not possible to have wisdom, for wisdom only comes by His Spirit. Only God can face us down and tell us what he really thinks about things that we think are fine, but that he detests.

If our priority is the things of this world, then we won't draw near to God; but if we seek God above all else, it's possible to find him, and he will lovingly supply what we need.

I've had some serious discussions with my wife about this concept. When Marina married me, I had several prosperous businesses, including a large farm, a big herd of cattle, and even a couple of airplanes along with substantial debt (see Rescue the Captors I, II and III, Russell Stendal, Life Sentence Publishing). I gave a tithe off the top of all my income and an even bigger percentage of my time to the Lord; sometimes I gave even larger financial offerings.

We came, however, to places along the way where we had to let go of many things in order to continue walking with the Lord. This wasn't always easy for Marina. For example, when I was kidnapped for the first time in 1983, my partner in the farming business took over running it, and by the time my captors released me, he had come to believe that the farm should belong to him. I knew the Lord was leading me down new paths. Instead of continuing to fight with my partner on the farm, I simply gave it to him (the assets as well as the debts) and walked away into the full-time ministry that the Lord has called me to ever since.

Marina and I were left with a small apartment and a diminutive car, but after a while I felt that we must sell even these and give the money away, because I could see that in the Lord's eyes there were some problems with the way in which I had acquired them. My wife was very upset. She didn't want me to get rid of either the apartment or the car, arguing that since she wasn't to blame for whatever I had done (which I had felt to be in good faith) in the past, she shouldn't be punished by losing her home and her means of independent transport. After even more time in prayer, I felt the Lord wanted me to leave things in his hands and not do anything drastic until Marina could accept it.

About three weeks later, she told me to go ahead with whatever the Lord was showing me to do, because she would be at peace with it. I sold our apartment and car and gave away the money, and true to her word, Marina was calm, trusting in God. The Lord then sent us, by faith, from Bogota, Colombia, to the Canadian Arctic and Alaska, where I spoke across the north for ten winters in a row, returning to minister all across Colombia the rest of the time. During this time of service, God provided for our needs every step along the way. As the ministry in Colombia has expanded, we have spent less time ministering in North America. God has given us wonderful children and grandchildren, excellent friends and coworkers, a new generation of young people on fire for God in Colombia, and many places all over the world that we may call home.

Do you remember the discussion between Jesus and Peter in Mark 10:28-30?

> *Then Peter began to say unto him, Behold,*
> *we have left all and have followed thee.*
> *And answering him, Jesus said, Verily I*
> *say unto you, There is no one that has left*
> *house or brethren or sisters or father or*
> *mother or wife or children or lands for my*
> *sake and the gospel's who shall not receive*
> *one hundredfold now in this time: houses*
> *and brethren and sisters and mothers and*
> *children and lands, with persecutions,*
> *and in the world to come eternal life.*

All of this has happened to us, including the ongoing persecution, because the Lord allows everyone that follows him to be tested and proven in every way and regarding every single thing.

Sometimes I sit down with my wife, and we thank the Lord for all of his wonderful provision. Marina has not yet experienced many of these places and events because she was not with me when I made some of those Canadian or European or African journeys, but as we have sought the kingdom of God and his righteousness, many blessings have been added unto us. For instance, those who belong to the worldwide family of God received us with open arms. As I searched the high Andes Mountains for remote transmitter locations so the Word of God could be broadcast by radio, we were given the use of, or sometimes even the outright ownership of, places and things that most people would not believe even if I were to tell them. Some of these sites are not very accessible and may not have much commercial value, but the people involved are very dear to the heart of God. For the most part, people of North American background are still not welcome to visit these beautiful places, but God has caused many of our enemies to come and make peace with us. They've even called on us to help make peace between warring factions.

Returning to Proverbs:

> 6 *For the LORD gives wisdom; out of his*
> *mouth comes knowledge and intelligence.*

If the Lord does not reveal himself, we cannot know him. If he does not communicate with us, we cannot understand. Knowledge and intelligence flow out of his mouth.

*7 He keeps the person of the upright; he is
a buckler to those that walk perfectly,*

The religious system has taught us that we can never be perfect; if it's impossible for us to *walk perfectly*, then this verse would make no sense because God would never be able to be a buckler (a shield) unto us. Leaders of the religious system may criticize us however they will, and in our natural state or on our own, we are unworthy, hopeless, and incapable of perfection. But Jesus Christ is upright and able to walk perfectly, and he desires to live inside us and to reign and rule in us and through us.

Many do not have him as their buckler/shield; such people must run and retreat in the face of adversity. If the Lord is our shield, however, everything that the enemy throws against us will come back upon the enemy. Scripture mentions the shield of faith (Ephesians 6:16), and yes, we are given a *measure* of faith; but when we surrender to the correction, discipline, and chastening of God, he then allows us to move forward in the unlimited faith of Jesus.

*8 keeping the paths of judgment and the
way of his merciful ones.*

Some prefer to remove the word *judgment* from the Bible because they think it's too negative. As a result, this and other similar words have been thinned out in most modern Bible translations. These people fail to understand that if we voluntarily allow God to judge us and to abolish in us that which he does not approve, then the other side of the coin appears – when the righteous are judged, they are rewarded. The reward of the righteous is not only eternal life; they are joint heirs with Jesus Christ.

Note this: Judgment, in order to be effective, must be accomplished by God. All that we are required to do is submit to his chastening and have mercy on others. Jesus said, *Blessed are the merciful, for they shall obtain mercy* (Matthew 5:7).

> 9 *Then shalt thou understand righteousness and judgment and equity, yea, every good path.*

Righteousness and *justice* are the same word in Hebrew. Righteousness is not something that we can accomplish on our own. Righteousness (or justice) is primarily a way of being, and it only comes from God. Righteousness is being what God wants us to be, so that we will be able to do what he wants us to do.

Equity means having a favorable balance: being fair and unbiased. The natural man is unable to apply judgment without going from one extreme to another. Apart from God, he will always go in a zigzag that will become more and more pronounced.

Most countries in the world have problems with their laws and their courts; there is such a thing as extradition as well, and there's even a world court. Yet few understand righteousness (justice), judgment, and equity. The only way we can have these qualities is if there are clean people; the only way to have clean people is if God cleanses them; and the only way that God will cleanse them is if they submit to him.

10 *When wisdom enters into thine heart and knowledge is sweet unto thy soul,*

11 *discretion shall preserve thee, intelligence shall keep thee*

12 *to deliver thee from the evil way, from the man that speaks perversion,*

13 *who leave the paths of uprightness to walk in the ways of darkness,*

14 *who rejoice to do evil and delight in wicked perversion,*

15 *whose ways are crooked, and they are crooked in their paths;*

Wisdom may enter into our hearts, but the knowledge that is sweet unto our soul is not primarily the knowledge that is brokered at most institutions of higher learning. This soul-sweet knowledge refers primarily to knowing God.

The discretion that will preserve us comes from the Spirit of God. His intelligence will keep us and even flow through us if we remain in tune with him. He is the only one who can deliver us from the evil way and from the man that speaks perversion. In our natural state, we are the man that speaks perversion, and only God can deliver us from ourselves.

It's not even possible for us to understand the difference between the paths of uprightness and the ways of darkness – not until we have been redeemed and delivered out of the darkness and into God's marvelous light. Only after we are in the light do we notice the true dimensions and extent of the grotesque perversion and darkness all around us.

> 16 *to deliver thee from the strange woman, even from the stranger who flatters with her words,*
>
> 17 *who forsakes the prince of her youth and forgets the covenant of her God.*
>
> 18 *Therefore her house inclines unto death, and her paths unto the dead.*
>
> 19 *None that go unto her return again, neither do they take hold of the paths of life.*
>
> 20 *That thou may walk in the way of good men and keep the paths of righteousness.*
>
> 21 *For the upright shall dwell in the land, and the perfect shall remain in it.*
>
> 22 *But the wicked shall be cut off from the earth, and the transgressors shall be rooted out of it.*

All of this truth is applicable on several different levels. Israel, as a nation (and remember that the people of God are always symbolized by a woman in Bible prophecy), forsook the prince of her youth and forgot her covenant with God. Vast sectors of the church have also entered into prolonged apostasy for many centuries.

Anyone who is joined to a religious group that is not in a right relationship with God needs deliverance. This errant group will take them and their families down paths of death. Those who go unto her do not return.

True wisdom from God is required if we are to walk in the way of good men. Unless we receive the chastening of the Lord, it is not possible for us to be upright, and only the upright shall dwell in the land. *Perfection* is the same word as *maturity* in Hebrew. Only those who have come to maturity (only the perfect) shall remain in the land. Jesus Christ is perfect. He is mature. Only those in Christ by faith are sons of God; these are the ones God will discipline, correct, chasten, and bless as he sees fit.

The wicked shall be cut off from the earth. In Scripture, the earth is symbolic of the people of God – Israel and the church. The transgressors are the ones to be *rooted out* from among the people of God. At the time of the harvest, it is the tares that shall be removed first from among the wheat and not the other way around (Matthew 13:37-43).

The *strange woman* would have us believe that the people of God will be raptured away to heaven and that the wicked and the transgressors shall be left for a certain period of time upon the earth. Nothing could be further from the truth. It is the upright who shall dwell in the land; it is the perfect who shall remain in it.

Let Us Pray:

Lord, we thank you for the liberty that we have, that enables us to follow the voice of wisdom at the prompting of your Spirit. We thank you for keeping us and for delivering us from the strange woman. May we walk in the way of good men and keep the paths of righteousness. Amen.

Chapter 3

God Gives Grace unto the Humble

Proverbs 3

1 My son, forget not my law, but let thine heart keep my commandments:

2 For they shall add length of days and long life and peace unto thee.

This is the wisdom of God speaking, and it is addressed to *my son*. Not to slaves, not to servants, but to the sons (and daughters) who are the heirs. God loves his children, and he chastens us; he takes the time and trouble to correct and guide us. In our mind, we are to follow the law of God and not forget it, but it is with our heart that we keep his commandments.

3 Let not mercy and truth forsake thee; bind them about thy neck; write them upon the tablet of thine heart:

4 So shalt thou find grace and good favour in the sight of God and man.

Mercy and truth are paired; as we are aligned with the truth (through the discipline and chastening of God), we obtain mercy; as we show mercy, we shall also obtain it. In the New Covenant, God promises to write his commandments on the tablets of our hearts and in our minds. In verse three we are asked to bind mercy and truth about our neck and write them upon the tablet of our heart. Mercy without truth is not balanced. Mercy balanced with truth is the key to finding grace and good favor in the sight of God and man. I'm sure you remember this description of the young Jesus in Luke 2:51-52: *And he went down with them and came to Nazareth and was subject unto them, but his mother kept all these things in her heart. And Jesus increased in wisdom and in age and in grace with God and men.*

In his earthly life, Jesus showed us how to live totally in alignment with God, and the wisdom he demonstrated even at a young age was in line with the wisdom described in Proverbs.

> 5 *Trust in the LORD with all thine heart and lean not unto thine own understanding.*

> 6 *In all thy ways acknowledge him, and he shall direct thy paths.*

If we're to walk in the wisdom of God, we must not depend upon our own understanding. If we trust (or depend) upon the Lord (instead of ourselves) with all of our heart and place him first in everything, he will direct our paths. He will show us how and where to go. Scripture also states that *the steps of a good man are ordered by the LORD* (Psalm 37:23). It's simply not possible to walk in righteousness unless we're walking as God directs.

God is eager to direct our steps, but first we must desire in our hearts to know his will and to understand his wisdom and his ways; then he can and will speak to us through our hearts. If we allow him to uproot all our wrong thoughts and desires, he'll place his thoughts and his desires within us.

Those who rely on their own understanding to distill moral values and precepts from the Bible and apply them, receive their direction and counsel from other people instead of from God, and make their decisions based on fear of man or fear of circumstances (instead of in the fear of the Lord) will all be deceived and become self-righteous.

> 7 *Be not wise in thine own eyes; fear the LORD and depart from evil.*
>
> 8 *It shall be medicine to thy navel and marrow to thy bones.*

The best preventative medicine that exists is to fear the Lord and depart from evil. If we allow the Lord to order our steps and live to please him, then he will cause us to be strong and healthy in the midst of a cruel and corrupt world.

> 9 *Honour the LORD with thy substance and with the firstfruits of all thine increase.*
>
> 10 *So shall thy barns be filled with plenty,*

*and thy presses shall burst out with new
wine.*

This book does not mention tithes but rather first-
fruits. According to this verse, we are to honor God
with all of our substance. If Jesus is the pattern Son
who will receive the fullness of the inheritance, then
according to the New Testament, all of those who are
in a right relationship with him are firstfruits unto
God and members of the body of Christ (James 1:18;
Revelation 14:4). His barns (congregations) will then
be filled with plenty, and his presses will burst out with
new wine (with new life).

This is all subverted when the leaders of churches
and congregations take tithes and offerings (not to
mention people) unto themselves and fail to ensure that
the people are directly under the discipline, correction,
and chastening of God. Consequently, in many places,
particularly in North America and Western Europe,
the barns are not filled with plenty, and the presses are
not bursting out with new wine.

> 11 *My son, do not despise the chasten-
> ing of the LORD; neither be weary of his
> correction:*
>
> 12 *For the LORD chastens whom he loves
> and delights in, even as a father to his son.*

Remember that chastening is for the purpose of
making us chaste, or clean and pure, so we can come
to maturity (or perfection) in Christ. In Hebrews 5:7-9,
Scripture has this to say regarding Jesus:

Who in the days of his flesh, when he had
offered up prayers and supplications with
strong crying and tears unto him that was
able to save him from death, was heard
because of his reverent fear; although he
was the Son of God, yet he learned obedi-
ence by the things which he suffered; and
being made perfect, he became the author
of eternal saving health unto all those that
hearken unto him,

Scripture says that we're to hearken unto the chastening of our father (Proverbs 1:8). This is true regarding
our natural father but even more important regarding
our heavenly Father. Chastening is something that
begins with a word (advice or guidance) that can be
hearkened unto (heard and obeyed). Adam was told
not to touch a certain tree, and the consequences of
his disobedience were death and the fall. Jesus was told
to die upon a tree, and the consequences of his obedience were life and redemption for an entire fallen race.

13 *Blessed is the man that has found wis-*
dom and who brings to light intelligence,

14 *for the merchandise of it is better than*
the merchandise of silver and the fruits
thereof more than fine gold.

15 *She is more precious than precious*
stones, and all the things thou canst desire
are not to be compared unto her.

16 *Length of days is in her right hand and in her left hand riches and honour.*

17 *Her ways are ways of pleasantness, and all her paths are peace.*

18 *She is a tree of life to those that lay hold upon her, and blessed is every one that retains her.*

19 *The LORD by wisdom has founded the earth; by intelligence has he established the heavens.*

The consequences of seeking wisdom are the same as those of seeking the kingdom of God and his righteousness – if we find wisdom, everything else will be added unto us.

The tree of life represents Jesus, through whom God created the heavens and the earth. To find wisdom is to find Jesus Christ. Jesus also desires to work in and through us until the life of Christ flowing in and through us produces the fruit of the Holy Spirit. In the first creation, he made the seeds before any plants or trees actually grew (Genesis 2:4-5). In the new creation, Jesus is the seed, and he desires to plant his life into us and have it flourish. In the book of Revelation, the tree of life grows in the plaza of the city and on both banks of the river (Revelation 22:2).

The body of Christ is typed as female (the bride of Christ), and Jesus is the head of the body. The word *wisdom* is feminine in the Hebrew language and therefore is typed as female in the book of Proverbs. This is because the wisdom of God will flow through the entire body of Christ, starting from Jesus, the head, and streaming in and through every member of the body (Ephesians 4:15-16). By the Spirit, Paul painted a wonderful word picture of this in Colossians 1:16-20 when he wrote:

> *by him were all things created, that are in the heavens and that are in the earth, visible and invisible whether they are thrones or dominions or principalities or powers: all things were created by him and in him, And he is before all things, and by him all things consist. And he is the head of the body, the congregation, who is the beginning, the firstborn from the dead, that in all things he might have the preeminence. For it please the Father that in him should all fullness dwell and by him to reconcile all things unto himself, having made peace through the blood of his cross, whether they are the things in the earth or the things in the heavens.*

Before wisdom can flow through us, however, Proverbs tell us that a little spade work is often necessary.

> *20 By his knowledge the depths are broken up, and the heavens drop down dew.*

The depths that are broken up include the hardness of our hearts; when this hardness is shattered and we submit to God's chastening, then his clean word from heaven will descend on us like dew. As Jesus said, *Blessed are the pure in heart for they shall see God* (Matthew 5:8). If our hearts are pure, we will be able to see the wisdom and discretion of God. This will make all the difference between life and death in the coming judgment of Israel, the church, and the world.

> 21 *My son, do not let them depart from thine eyes; keep sound wisdom and discretion,*
>
> 22 *so shall they be life unto thy soul and grace to thy neck.*
>
> 23 *Then shalt thou walk in thy way safely, and thy foot shall not stumble.*
>
> 24 *When thou liest down, thou shalt not be afraid: yea, thou shalt lie down, and thy sleep shall be sweet.*
>
> 25 *Thou shalt not be afraid of sudden fear, neither of the desolation of the wicked when it comes.*
>
> 26 *For the LORD shall be thy confidence and shall keep thy foot from being taken.*

When Jesus returns, one shall be taken and another left. It shall be as in the days of Noah when the flood came and took away all of the wicked, leaving only righteous Noah and his family (eight souls) who were saved in the ark (Matthew 24:36-42).

> 27 *Do not withhold good from those to whom it is due, when it is in the power of thine hand to do it.*

28 *Do not say unto thy neighbor, Go and
come again and tomorrow I will give
when thou hast it by thee.*

29 *Do not devise evil against thy neighbor,
seeing he dwells securely by thee.*

30 *Do not sue a man without cause, if he
has done thee no harm.*

Human society is divided, and we are all too prone
to choose sides. There are many currents of right and
left wing politics, numerous economic blocks and inter-
ests, and myriad differences for one reason or another
among those claiming to be the people of God. But we
are to be, as much as possible, a blessing to all.

31 *Envy thou not the oppressor and choose
none of his ways.*

32 *For the perverse is an abomination
to the LORD; but his secret is with the
righteous.*

How many unjust leaders are oppressing the people
of God? How many great and powerful ministries are
really perverse abominations in the eyes of the Lord?

What is the secret of the Lord, the *secret* that is
with the righteous? It is a special place of security.
The Lord has secret plans that he only shares with his
friends – those who keep his commandments. And his
commandment is that we love God and one another.

33 *The curse of the LORD is in the house
of the wicked, but he shall bless the habitation of the just.*

The curse is presently in the house of the wicked. The entire earth is under this curse, and the Devil has been in charge for six millennia. But God shall bless the habitation of the just. When will the fullness of the promised blessing arrive? What is the habitation of the just?

In order for the fullness of the promise to come, the wicked must be removed from among the righteous. At present the earth is the habitation of both the just and the unjust. It must be cleansed by the judgments of God. Only then will it be the habitation of the just, and worthy to receive his blessing.

> 34 *Surely he scorns the scorners; but he gives grace unto the humble.*

> 35 *The wise shall inherit glory; but shame shall be the promotion of fools.*

Let Us Pray:

Heavenly Father, may we learn your ways. May you write your laws on the tablets of our hearts and in our minds. Please correct all our erroneous beliefs and bring us into a perfect balance of mercy and truth. Cause us to love your ways. May we keep our eyes fixed on your wisdom and discretion. We ask this in the name of our Lord Jesus Christ. Amen.

Chapter 4

Above All Else,
Guard Thy Heart

Proverbs 4

1 Hearken, ye sons, unto the chastening of the father, and pay attention that ye might know understanding.

2 For I give you good doctrine; do not forsake my law.

The children of Israel received the law of Moses and the Ten Commandments written on tablets of stone in the wilderness with Moses acting as an intermediary, because they were afraid to hear the voice of God for themselves (Exodus 20:19). The New Covenant is the law written not on tablets of stone but on the tablets of our hearts and in our minds. Those who are led by the Spirit of God are the sons of God and are not under the (external) law. They are ruled by the law of the Spirit of life, which sets us free from the law of sin and death (Romans 8:2). This is the law of liberty (James 1:25; 2:12), and where the Spirit of the Lord is, there is liberty to do the will of God (2 Corinthians 3:17).

> 3 *For I was my father's son, tender and*
> *unique in the sight of my mother.*

Natural fathers and mothers have God-given responsibility for a certain season, until their children reach maturity (Ephesians 6:1). Our heavenly Father, however, will always have the ultimate authority. If we are born again from above, Scripture states that "the Jerusalem of above" is the mother of us all (Galatians 4:26).

> 4 *He taught me and said unto me, Sustain*
> *thine heart with my words; keep my com-*
> *mandments, and live.*

God, who can reveal himself in many ways, has chosen in these last times to speak to us through his Son, Jesus Christ, who desires to dwell in our hearts if we will receive him (Hebrews 1:1-2). Only after our hearts submit to the chastening and correction of Father God, however, will it be possible to bring every thought and imagination captive to the Lord Jesus.

When the Lord cleanses our heart, then our feelings and motivation are affected. Our conscience becomes more and more sensitive. We begin to sense the heart of God as his love and wisdom and understanding start to permeate our being. He begins to write his commandments in our hearts and then in our minds. It requires an intellectual leap of faith to walk with God, but we can rest assured that all our questions and our intrigue will be resolved later, along the way.

> 5 *Get wisdom, get understanding; forget it*

not; neither decline from the words of r
mouth.

6 Forsake her not, and she shall preserve
thee; love her, and she shall keep thee.

Wisdom and understanding begin in our hearts, and from the fullness of our hearts, our mouths speak.

7 Wisdom is the principal thing, therefore
get wisdom: and with all thy getting get
understanding.

8 Grow in wisdom, and she shall promote
thee; she shall bring thee to honour when
thou hast embraced her.

9 She shall give to thine head an increase
of grace; a crown of glory shall she deliver
to thee.

If Jesus is our head, the increase of grace and the crown of glory will be for him (Revelation 4:10-11).

Only as we're able to hear his words directly from him will we be granted the grace to do his will. This is how we're able to keep his commandments and live. God desires to speak with us on a direct and personal basis, yet many people are confused and have great difficulty discerning the voice of God because they try to hear with their minds instead of with their hearts.

We must begin by trusting from the heart; otherwise, our intellect will get in the way and may block us from knowing God and establishing a close friendship with him. We are to come as a little child. Amazingly enough, the way to God is so simple that even a child or a mentally challenged person can respond to his love, while those who consider themselves to be wise may have a much more difficult time.

We're surrounded by a world and an educational system run by intellectuals who seem to think they can advance from course to course and from diploma to diploma by sheer mental capacity, which may be true in terms of worldly knowledge. God says, however, that unless we know him from the heart, it is impossible to obtain true wisdom.

> 10 *Hear, O my son, and receive my*
> *words, and the years of thy life shall be*
> *multiplied.*

It's easy to understand how some years might be added to our lives as we learn to listen to the voice of God, but what if the years of our life were not just added but multiplied? How could this be? Well, remember that Scripture states in Revelation 20:4-5 that there will be a first resurrection: *And I saw thrones, and those who sat upon them and judgment was given unto them; and I saw the souls of those that were beheaded for the witness of Jesus and for the word of God and who had not worshipped the beast neither its image neither had received its mark upon their foreheads or in their hands; and they shall live and reign with Christ the thousand years. But the rest of the dead did not live again until the thousand years were finished. This is the first resurrection.*

In the wisdom of God, those who have been *beheaded* for the witness of Jesus are not necessarily limited to those faithful to God who have fallen into the hands of those like ISIS. Rather, they are those who have come under his headship and authority and have submitted to his chastening. Those who have the mark of the beast (of the natural, carnal man) in their foreheads or in their hands are those who think and act according to the fallen nature of Adam.

> 11 *I have taught thee in the way of wisdom;*
> *I have caused thee to walk in right paths.*

The way of wisdom is when God orders our steps. God will cause us to walk in right paths if we submit to his doctrine and teaching.

> 12 *When thou goest in these paths, thy*
> *steps shall not be hindered; and when*
> *thou runnest, thou shalt not stumble.*

> 13 *Take fast hold of chastening; do not let*
> *go; keep this; for it is thy life.*

Sometimes we wonder if we're being punished unjustly or facing unnecessary adversity, when God is working behind the scenes to cleanse our hearts and order our steps. If we have patience and faith, we'll discover along the way that all of this has been for our good. If we embrace the chastening and correction of our heavenly Father, he will control every detail of our existence. He will use any person, any factor, any situation to bring about his purposes in our lives.

> 14 *Enter not into the path of the wicked,*
> *and go not in the way of evil men.*

> 15 *Avoid it, pass not by it, turn from it,*
> *and pass away.*

When we are walking on the spiritual path and

come to a fork in the road, we have the possibility of taking the path of the wicked or continuing on the way of the righteous. There are many such crossings, and sometimes it's hard to tell which way to go. Many may desire to be our fellow travelers, but only God knows the status of their hearts. At times like this, only the wisdom, discernment, and understanding that come from God will suffice.

> 16 *For they do not sleep, unless they have done evil; and their sleep is taken away, unless they cause someone to fall.*
>
> 17 *For they eat the bread of wickedness, and drink the wine of violence.*

When our conscience is tuned to God and we do something bad (or fail to follow the prompting of the Holy Spirit), we will not be able to sleep, because the Lord desires us to stop, turn around, and return to his ways. However, those who continually violate their conscience come to the place where they not only cease to hear their conscience but are actually sustained by evil. They can't sleep unless they've caused someone to fall. They feed on wickedness and on violence.

> 18 *But the path of the just is as the light of the morning star, that shines more and more until the day is perfect.*
>
> 19 *The way of the wicked is darkness; they do not know in what they stumble.*

As the wicked become worse and worse, so focused on their evil plans that they can't see the trap that will cause them to stumble, the righteous shine brighter and brighter as the new day of God dawns.

> 20 *My son, attend to my words; incline thine ear unto my words.*

> 21 *Let them not depart from thine eyes; keep them in the midst of thine heart.*

> 22 *For they are life unto those that find them and medicine to all their flesh.*

> 23 *Above all else, guard thy heart; for out of it flows the issues of life.*

It appears that King David wrote the first nine chapters of the book of Proverbs for his son, Solomon. But in spite of all his famous wisdom, Solomon didn't really continue to guard his heart according to the petition of his father (1 Chronicles 29:19). Instead, he let his desires go after pagan women, and they caused his heart to turn away from the Lord (1 Kings 11:1-13).

It does appear that Solomon repented near the end of his life when he wrote the book of Ecclesiastes, but the consequences of his earlier apostasy were devastating. His behavior ended the golden age of Israel. The abominations initiated by Solomon on high places at the insistence of his wives were not abolished and torn down until the reign of King Josiah, almost five hundred years later on the eve of the Babylonian captivity.

> 24 *Put away from thee the perversion of the mouth, and the deviation of the lips put far from thee.*

> 25 *Let thine eyes look upon that which is*

*right, and let thine eyelids straighten thy
path before thee.*

*26 Ponder the path of thy feet, and let all
thy ways be established.*

*27 Turn not to the right hand nor to the
left; remove thy foot from evil.*

There are many who calculate: What's the minimum I can do and still be saved?

I wish them the best and hope that they make it. God is not willing that any should perish. He desires everyone to come to repentance and salvation. For those who opt for the minimum, I have a question: What if you've miscalculated?

Isn't it preferable to heed sound advice and guard our hearts above all else? Isn't it much better to put away perversion of the mouth and put deviation of the lips far from us? Should we not do much better to focus our gaze upon that which is right and let our eyelids straighten our path before us? Shouldn't we ponder the path of our feet and let all of our ways be established by the Lord? Then we won't turn either to the right or to the left of the perfect will of God for our lives.

Let Us Pray:

Heavenly Father, we give you thanks for your word; for your unfolding revelation; for the way you give us more and more clarity each day. Above all else, may we guard our hearts. May we always love your truth and your light above all else. We ask this in the name of our Lord Jesus Christ. Amen.

Chapter 5

Thy Fountain Shall Be Blessed

Proverbs 5

*1 My son, attend unto my wisdom, and
bow thine ear to my intelligence;*

The New Testament says that *faith comes by hearing, and the ear to hear by the word of God*
(Romans 10:17).

*2 that thou may keep council and that thy
lips may conserve knowledge.*

The world that surrounds us has deceived us in many
ways. Many believe that knowledge is something that
man can derive from the scientific method, but this
method itself is used by fallen man, who tends (often
unconsciously) to manipulate the available evidence
in a way that supports his existing concepts and phi-
losophy. Proverbs tells us that unless we attend to the
wisdom of God and bow to his intelligence, we will not
be able to keep council (the archaic use of this word

means we will not be able to make determinations and decisions that we will be able to stand with over time) and conserve true knowledge. Entire branches of modern science, however, appear to have lost the knowledge of God.

In some branches of what man calls science, it's more or less easy to know if a mistake is being made or not. "Hard" sciences such as physics or chemistry involve a high degree of accuracy, objectivity, and replicability.

Other areas, however, such as the so-called social sciences or "soft" sciences where things are often more abstract and arbitrary. A high percentage of research results in published scientific articles in these fields but is unable to be duplicated by peer scientists using the same data. This even applies to modern Bible translations; with the advent of modern textual criticism, the translator can search at his or her discretion between variant and even deviant manuscripts and take the rendition that makes more sense according to that person's intellectual criteria or academic formation.

True knowledge or true science is not like this. True knowledge has to do with how things really are and how they really function in relation to God. When man errs in science, sometimes it takes a long time to discover the depth of the error. Some scientists tend to be arrogant and fight with one another over who discovered something first or who had the better ideas. Many times what is only a hypothesis is presented as full-fledged theory or even as fact. A series of impeccably logical "scientific" steps or stages can be based on an assumption that turns out to have been fatally flawed. Then the conclusions are meaningless.

The great scientific advances and revelations that have bettered society, even in technology, overwhelmingly came from scientists with a Jewish or Christian background (men and women who operate in some degree of fear or awe of the Lord).

Another source of knowledge exists, but that one is a tainted one. Satan began his rebellion against God by presenting lies as knowledge. Some of his deadly lies have a very high percentage of truth, and there's a reason for this. Did you know that rat poison is ninety-nine percent rat food? That's because otherwise the rats wouldn't be so foolish as to kill themselves eating it. Satan deceived Eve by telling her plausible-sounding lies and then used her to get Adam to rebel against God. After Eve was compromised, Adam was forced to choose between her and God.

King David – who learned the hard way about the dangers of a *strange* woman – wants to use these proverbs to warn his son, Solomon, about such risks. It was a woman who was almost the downfall of David, but despite his father's example, the sound advice he received as a youth, and his own well-known, God-given wisdom as an adult, Solomon didn't learn this lesson for himself until near the end of his life. Even after all the warnings of his father, King Solomon had far too many dealings with strange women, starting early when he married Pharaoh's daughter, and the consequences of this for the nation of Israel were irreversible. All of the legendary wisdom that Solomon received from God was unable to thwart the plans of the enemy, simply because Solomon failed to guard his heart above all else.

My father always taught me that learning from the mistakes of others can save us from being caught in the same error. The lessons described in the Bible, so often learned through pain, are written for our benefit.

> 3 *For the lips of the strange woman*
> *drop as a honeycomb, and her mouth is*
> *smoother than oil,*
>
> 4 *But her end is bitter as wormwood,*
> *sharp as a twoedged sword.*
>
> 5 *Her feet go down to death, her steps*
> *uphold Sheol,*

Sheol (or Hades, in Greek) is linked to the first death – the one that can kill the body but not the soul. Hell, the lake of fire, is the second death, and it can destroy both the body and the soul (Matthew 10:28). This second death, which is mentioned five times in Revelation, is the sentence of eternal perdition upon the wicked at the final judgment. Hades must give up her dead when that final judgment takes place (Revelation 20:13-15).

The Devil had the keys to Sheol and was able to imprison (with very few exceptions) every human soul in death after Adam ceded his God-given dominion and the entire creation became frustrated and under the curse. When Jesus died, however, he descended into Sheol and led captivity captive; then he ascended on high with those who were his (Ephesians 4:8-10). Now

Jesus holds the keys of Hades and of death (Revelation 1:18), and soon he will imprison Satan for a thousand years (Revelation 20:1-3) in what used to be his own jail.

Although it may be argued that Adam would not have behaved this way had it not been for Eve, Scripture blames the fall not on Eve but on Adam (Romans 5:14; 1 Timothy 2:14). Eve was beguiled by a strange word, a concept that did not come from God, and this caused her to change her attitude toward God and become estranged from him. Then Adam, with his eyes wide open, chose to follow Eve rather than God. This was rebellion against the Creator.

Scripture many times uses a woman to symbolize an entire people or congregation. On a metaphorical level, we are told that Jesus Christ will have a bride without spot or wrinkle, and his bride (his people) will not repeat the fatal mistake of Eve. And on a literal and carnal level, it's certainly possible for men to be seduced by *strange* women. However, the only way that this and similar passages can apply to both men and women is if we realize that there are many *strange* congregations or groups out there that have succumbed to the lies of the Devil instead of walking in the truth of God.

The woman in these verses, representing a religious congregation is not clean: she is full of abominations. She is responsible for the blood shed by all the righteous and all the saints who have been slain (Revelation 17:4-6; 18:24). And she has many daughters.

The true congregation of born-again believers form the true bride of Christ; but Scripture also defines the synagogue of Satan (Revelation 2:9). This "synagogue" is a very religious congregation that appears to be of God when in fact it is of Satan.

The true congregation, the clean woman, does not have a headquarters here on earth. If we are born from above and if God is our Father, the mother of us all is the "Jerusalem from above," the free Jerusalem, (Galatians 4:26). Therefore, if we're born again into the great congregation of the new heavenly Jerusalem, our citizenship will not be from this earth. We will be citizens and dwellers of heavenly places in Christ, even while we walk here upon the earth. When the great tribulation of the judgments of God falls, Scripture advises us to *rejoice ye heavens and ye that dwell in them* (Revelation 12:12).

Revelation is full of warnings to those who name the name of God yet are categorized as "dwellers of the earth." Those who seek the things of this earth are earthly; those who seek the things above are heavenly. We have the opportunity, during our sojourn here upon the earth, to invest our resources. We may invest in that which is earthly or in that which will yield heavenly dividends. We may invest in our physical comfort here upon the earth in accordance with the culture that surrounds us, or we may invest our time and resources in accordance with the leading of the Holy Spirit.

> 6 *lest thou should ponder the path of life,*
> *her ways are unstable; thou shalt not*
> *know them.*
>
> 7 *Hear me now therefore, O ye sons, and*
> *do not depart from the words of my mouth.*

> 8 *Remove thy way far from her, and do*
> *not come near the door of her house,*

The door of the woman's house may be a church, a congregation, or a financial institution where they give you advice about how to obtain the things of this world in exchange for including them in your budget. Many of us do things like that instead of simply placing everything into the hands of the Lord and allowing him to lead and guide us regarding the investment of our time and resources.

> 9 *lest thou give thine honour unto others*
> *and thy years unto the cruel,*

> 10 *lest strangers be filled with thy wealth,*
> *and thy labours be in the house of a*
> *stranger,*

This is even worse than having an affair with a lover outside of marriage (which is extremely serious and has the same type of consequences). Those who split off from the true family of God and insert themselves into a congregation that is not of God will lose all of their time, money, and effort.

Ecumenicalism, unity between different churches, sounds admirable in theory. *Ecumenical* means "in the family," and who could object to family unity? There are, however, only two families that matter – Adam's family and Christ's family. Sadly, many are attempting to come together in Adam instead of in Christ.

> 11 *and thou mourn at the last when thy*
> *flesh and thy body are consumed*

12 *and say, How have I hated chastening*
and my heart despised reproof

13 *and have not obeyed the voice of those*
who chastened me, nor inclined my ear to
those that instructed me!

If the Spirit of God is not present, there will be precious little chastening, reproof, or instruction. Instead, there will be very gifted and highly educated men and women who are using their God-given gifts to amass personal or corporate power and gain.

14 *I have been in almost every kind of*
evil in the midst of society and of the
congregation.

If the direct chastening of Father God is exchanged for the correction and discipline of men, a chaste society or a chaste congregation will never be formed.

15 *Drink waters out of thine own cistern*
and running waters out of thine own well.

16 *Let thy fountains be dispersed abroad,*
and rivers of thy waters in the streets.

17 *Let them be only thine own and not for*
strangers with thee.

On the surface this appears to be speaking of the virtues of marriage, reminding us that we must be content with our own wife and family. This is all true.

Beyond this meaning, and even deeper, is that once the Lord has placed his Spirit in each one of us, we don't have to consult other people in order to receive our leading and guidance from God and our intimate communion with him. After all, if we had to consult and trust prophets, pastors, elders, or spiritual directors for each step that we're to make, this concept would have been written in the gospel, because Jesus' earthly life is the model for all of us.

Can you imagine any book in the Bible containing scenes like these?

> "Peter, tell me: did you have a dream last night? Did any of you have a vision? We need to confirm our plans for tomorrow."

> "John, I need to know: do you have a prophecy or a word of knowledge or wisdom?"

> "Lazarus just died, and I have to make an important decision. Should we go or not go?"

> "We need to confirm our travel plans in the mouth of two or three witnesses. What do you guys think?"

No! Nothing like this ever went on anywhere in the New Testament.

Jesus, on the vast majority of occasions, made life-or-death decisions without even registering a formal, verbal prayer to his heavenly Father. The Jubilee Bible uses the 500-year-old common English of William Tyndale, and this is what the word *council* means here in the book of Proverbs when applied to an individual (Proverbs 1:4; 5:2). Jesus was in direct heart-to-heart communion with his Father by means of the Spirit; therefore, he always felt and knew his Father's heart.

This is true knowledge. Absolutely no evidence exists that Jesus was led by external guidance or by the gifting of others. He never taught his disciples to seek apostles or prophets or elders or others for confirmation. Clearly, Jesus was moved from the heart, and his heart was always linked with his heavenly Father. Jesus was the temple of the Father, and the Father dwelt in him by the Spirit. His prayer and commandment was that we would love one another and become one with him, just as he and the Father are – and always were – one (John 17:11, 20-23).

> 15 *Drink waters out of thine own cistern*
> *and running waters out of thine own well.*

Our own cistern is our personal and direct relationship with Jesus. Running waters are living waters: they're our source of life by the Spirit. And the Holy Spirit that our Lord places in us is our well from which we can draw those running, living waters.

Marriage also symbolizes this union, when two individuals become one flesh.

> 16 *Let thy fountains be dispersed abroad,*
> *and rivers of thy waters in the streets.*

> 17 *Let them be only thine own and not for*
> *strangers with thee.*

The Holy Spirit fills us with these rivers of the water of life, and they will then flow from the most intimate parts of our being. The Spirit flows from our hearts and reveals the feelings and thoughts of God. This allows us to make instantaneous decisions that line up exactly with the will of God – as long as our hearts are clean and pure. This isn't a game of mental arithmetic where our calculations must be compared and checked out with other sources to see if they're valid. There is no room for strangers in our intimate communion with God, just as there is no room for strangers in our marriage bed.

Solomon had enjoyed that intimate communion with God, who had given him great gifts of wisdom; and when God gives a gift, he will not remove it immediately if the person makes wrong or even perverse use of it, as Solomon did. He ultimately loved "many strange women" who *turned away his heart after other gods* to such an extent that *his heart was not perfect with the Lord his God* (1 Kings 11:4). With all of his wisdom, Solomon forgot that gifts and ministries are intended to flow from the heart of God so the people may be joined to the Lord and led by the heart and wisdom of God (Ephesians 4:11-16). This concept defies human intellect – even the intellect of a Solomon.

> 18 *Thy fountain shall be blessed; and*
> *rejoice with the wife of thy youth.*

This is all wonderful marriage advice. None of it, however, seems to have done Solomon (with all his famous wisdom) any good. He ended up with a thousand women, some from pagan nations with whom God had specifically forbidden marriage. His heart went in many directions and led him into severe apostasy.

It's worth noting here that human failings can't thwart God's plans. God had told Solomon that if he was faithful and followed in the footsteps of his father, King David, then God would confirm his kingdom, and there would never fail to be an heir of Solomon upon the throne of Israel (2 Chronicles 7:18). Tragically, Solomon didn't live up to this; but in spite of that apostasy, God kept his promises to David and brought forth the line of Christ. Note that the linage of Joseph recorded by Matthew goes through Solomon, but the linage of Mary recorded by Luke does not.

God desires to place his presence within us. He calls us to service and to a special relationship with him. Spiritually this is like the wife of our youth. When God gives us a wife, he doesn't want us to ever turn our back on her or diminish our commitment to her. And when God places a call of service and of ministry unto himself upon us, he desires for us to treat this call in the same manner.

> 19 *Let her be as the loving hind and pleas-*
> *ant roe; let her breasts satisfy thee at all*
> *times; and be thou ravished always with*
> *her love, without eyes for anyone else.*

In the natural realm, I know that the wife of my youth is the woman God gave me. The Lord has caused her to be a great blessing to me, but this goes even beyond that. The original has the connotation of being blind toward anyone else. I am to have eyes only for the wife that God gave me and never even think about looking to anyone else.

This is an example of how we are to be with our calling and place in God. We are to be married to the design and purpose of God for our lives. We may not find it easy, but if we ask for his help with this, God will support us in cleaving to his plans for us.

> 20 *And why wilt thou, my son, be ravished*
> *with a woman belonging to someone else,*
> *and embrace the bosom of a stranger?*

Regardless of whatever excuses they may make for their conduct, at heart those who do this are seeking fleeting pleasure, and temporary worldly gain instead of godliness.

> 21 *For the ways of man are before the eyes*
> *of the LORD, and he weighs all his goings.*

> 22 *His own iniquities shall take hold of*
> *the wicked, and he shall be imprisoned*
> *with the cords of his sins.*

The wicked one is the Devil, and all of his followers are wicked in the eyes of God. They did not esteem their first estate in the glory and purity of the direct presence of God, and many have followed their example, but in the end they cannot escape the consequences of their wrongdoing.

> 23 *He shall die because he did not submit*
> *to chastening; and due to the greatness of*
> *his folly he shall go astray.*

Some interesting parallels appear in Jude 3-6, which reads:

> *Beloved, when I gave all diligence to write*
> *unto you of the common salvation, it was*
> *needful for me to write unto you and*

*exhort you that ye should earnestly per-
severe in the faith which was given once
to the saints. For there are certain men
crept in unawares without fear or rever-
ence of God, who from beforehand have
been ordained unto this condemnation,
turning the grace of our God into lascivi-
ousness and denying God who alone has
dominion, and our Lord Jesus, the Christ.
I will, therefore, remind you, though ye
once knew this, how that the Lord, having
saved the people out of the land of Egypt,
afterward destroyed those that did not
believe. And the angels who did not keep
their first estate but left their own habitation, he has reserved in eternal chains
under darkness unto the judgment of the
great day.*

Any regular church attendee can notice the machi-
nations that go on in the congregations of men. Our
churches are full of problems of control, the ensuing
splits, and the disasters in the personal lives when
people place themselves under the control of intermediaries instead of under the hand of God the Father
for the discipline and chastening mentioned above in
verse 23. Like the *certain men* mentioned by Jude, they
are moved by the desire to save their own lives or by
ambitions of personal gain (of pleasure, power and/
or money) and fall prey to a religious spirit that is not

God. As a result, corruption multiplies, rather than the grace of God.

The religious spirit that is not God is really a demon passing himself off as an angel of light and operating potent gifts. The Devil still has great gifts that were given him by God, including a powerful ability to convince people to worship man and submit to one another instead of directly to God. But our calling and election is not to build a religious city here upon the earth. God took Abraham, the heir of the Promised Land, and showed him all of that land of promise; yet Abraham lived all his days in tents and made no continuing city, because he had a vision of a heavenly city with foundations, whose builder and maker is God (Hebrews 11:9-10).

Our job as Christians isn't to organize people so they depend upon us instead of upon God. Our mission is to walk with the Lord even if no one else will follow. The faith of each and every one will be tested. The Lord seeks hearts that are pure and clean, so he may join them to himself and to one another. He is the builder and maker of the city of God.

Proverbs warns us of the penalty we pay when we insist on going our own sinful way instead of yielding ourselves to God's chastening:

> 22 *His own iniquities shall take hold of the wicked, and he shall be imprisoned with the cords of his sins.*
>
> 23 *He shall die because he did not submit*

to chastening; and due to the greatness of
his folly he shall go astray.

Folly, especially great folly, is something we normally associate with mankind, but for the Devil to turn his back on his original estate or place in God was certainly a major act of folly, and he committed a greater piece of folly by beguiling Eve, the wife of Adam. Satan's plan was to disqualify Adam and take over Adam's responsibilities. It only partially worked, because even though Satan gained charge of this world, God cursed the earth and put enmity between Satan and the woman and promised that the seed of the woman (Christ) would bruise the head of the serpent (Satan).

By the time of Jesus, the Devil had completely taken over the vast majority of the leaders of the congregation, including almost all of the scribes, priests, Pharisees, and Sadducees (whom Jesus called sons of their father, the Devil). This turned the congregation that was supposed to be the people of God into a *strange woman*. Everyone who embraced her was eventually destroyed, and Satan lost all the sons that he had painstakingly planted in Jerusalem and who were using the temple (that they turned into a den of thieves) to sow lies and heresy all over the known world. Jesus used all of this to extend his presence all over the world through his new temple, the body of Christ. By the power of the Holy Spirit, the early church turned the world upside down.

The greatest folly of Satan and his followers, however, was their plan for the crucifixion of the Lord Jesus Christ, believing that if they could kill him, they would be able to hold him hostage by death in Sheol like they had been able to do with almost everyone else including the patriarchs. Instead, they played right into God's plan to offer his Son, Jesus, in atonement for the sins of the world. This re-created the bridge between God and man that had been broken in the garden of Eden. The Lord Jesus shattered forever the power of sin and death and took into his own possession the keys of death and Sheol, or Hades (Revelation 1:18). Soon the Devil's own iniquity and rebellion shall finally catch up with him. What he attempted to do to Jesus will happen to him, and he shall be bound for a thousand years in the bottomless pit, which is Hades (Revelation 20:1-2). After that, he shall be judged and cast into the lake of fire, which is eternal perdition, the second death (Revelation 20:10).

If Satan's acts have been folly, what is wisdom? Consider the description that Paul gives in 1 Corinthians 2:6-10.

> *For we speak perfect wisdom of God,*
> *and not the wisdom of this age nor of the*
> *princes of this age, that come to nought,*
> *but we speak the wisdom of God in a mys-*
> *tery, even the hidden wisdom, which God*
> *predestined before the ages unto our glory,*
> *which none of the princes of this age knew*
> *(for had they known it, they would never*
> *have crucified the Lord of glory). But as*
> *it is written, That which eye has not seen*
> *nor ear heard neither has entered into*

the heart of man is that which God has prepared for those that love him. But God has revealed this unto us by his Spirit, for the Spirit searches all things, even the deep things of God.

Let Us Pray:

Heavenly Father, we ask that you may chasten us and search out the depths of our hearts now, while there is still time. Please show us where we are making bad use of our time or of our resources. Please show us where we have things inverted or out of order. Please correct us and straighten us out so we may be found bearing good fruit at the time of the end. We ask this in the name of our Lord Jesus Christ. Amen.

Chapter 6

Escape as a Roe from the Hand of the Hunter

Proverbs 6

1 My son, if thou be surety for thy friend, if thou hast stricken thy hand with a stranger,

2 thou art snared with the words of thy mouth; thou art taken with the words of thy mouth.

3 Do this now, my son, and deliver thyself, for thou hast fallen into the hand of thy friend; go, humble thyself, and make sure thy friend.

4 Give not sleep to thine eyes, nor slumber to thine eyelids.

5 Escape as a roe from the hand of the hunter and as a bird from the hand of the fowler.

I don't know if this has happened to you, but at times when I've felt sorry for someone who was in need or listened to a sob story, the next moment I found myself mixed up in a mess. It's easy to listen to someone and then suddenly find ourselves responsible for something we should never have taken on or perhaps never even intended to. Some people are expert at placing the weight of their obligations on someone else.

How does this happen?

By a little slip of the tongue that can continue into a nightmare. This starts as an unforeseen snare, as a trap; but in order to defeat us, the enemy needs to get us to take deliberate wrong action.

Sometimes we might think that God wants us to provide surety for someone, just as there are times when we think we need someone to co-sign for us.

You cannot enter some places in Colombia today unless someone vouches for you. At one place where we went to hold some important meetings, the local person who received me said, "Look, this is the way that it is here: I must respond with my life for whatever you do or say in this area, and you must respond with your life for whoever you bring with you."

Let's look at those words in Proverbs again, and we'll see an even higher interpretation.

> 1 *My son ...*

This is speaking to sons of God.

> 1 *if thou be surety for thy friend, if thou hast stricken thy hand with a stranger,*

> 2 *thou art snared with the words of thy mouth; thou art taken with the words of thy mouth.*

In this scenario, there are friends and there are strangers. Only two trees matter: one gives good fruit and the other is corrupt. One tree will last forever, and the other will be cut down and destroyed. Some are friends of God and some are strangers to God. We must be very careful about vouching for strangers before our friends or vouching for our friends before strangers.

The entire race of Adam (natural man) has problems, yet individual people may be very cordial. If we treat them with respect and win their confidence, we may win them for the kingdom of God. We must remember where we've come from; we must bear in mind that if we're walking with the Lord, it's because the life of God is flowing inside of us to enable us to bear good fruit. This is a work of his grace.

But look at what can happen in ministry:

> Someone comes in and says, "Pastor, I don't feel saved."

> And the pastor responds reassuringly, "Of course you're saved. You're here with me as a member of this congregation. You went forward and prayed the sinner's prayer that we had you repeat. Of course you're saved."

God has dealt with me in times past for usurping his place in someone's life. The one to give tranquility and reassurance should be God. Jesus Christ is the only surety that any of us need. If he is behind us and flows through us when we open our mouth to tell someone else that the eternal state of their soul is safe and secure, then this is fine and well. But if that's not the case and we're speaking out of our own authority, we've now taken on a terrible responsibility. For this reason the Scripture states that each of us will give account before the judgment seat of Christ for every idle word that comes out of our mouth (Matthew 12:33-37).

The world is full of people who like to make judgments about others. In the Christian world, people seem to want to know and proclaim whether or not this or that person is saved. But it's a very serious business before the Lord to tell someone that the eternal state of their soul is fine if that isn't truly the case, and it's equally serious to say that someone isn't saved if they really are.

Many religious groups are on the lookout for someone who may not speak with their particular religious vocabulary, so they can pounce on that person and browbeat them into repeating a prayer or speaking in tongues or going through some other religious exercise such as being re-baptized. Instead of discerning the heart of others, these ostensibly faith-filled people only want to get each new person they encounter to jump through whatever religious hoops they've been trained to promote.

It's true that many people are lost and in desperate need of a personal encounter with Jesus Christ, but it's also true that we are not to judge another person's heart. We may observe others and see if the fruit of the Spirit is present, because God says we shall know them by their fruit (Matthew 7:20), but that doesn't necessarily mean that their religious trajectory and experience will – or even should – line up exactly with ours. We are explicitly ordered not to judge and not to condemn lest we be judged and condemned (Matthew 7:1).

I have encountered very gifted, talented ministers who could move multitudes and have rows of penitents lined up before the altars, yet their personal lives were so toxic and unclean and full of human control that the overall long-term effect was that of an abomination. It would be a serious matter if we were to become surety for such people. We should never vouch for anyone without a clear witness from the Holy Spirit. There are also those who would have us make a commitment – either to them or to one another – that would limit or interfere with our commitment and relationship with God. Obviously we are wise not to do so.

> 6 *Go to the ant, thou sluggard; consider her ways, and be wise,*
>
> 7 *Who having no guide, overseer, or ruler,*
>
> 8 *provides her food in the summer and gathers her food in the harvest.*

What does an ant have to do with all this?

How you feel about having *no guide, overseer, or ruler* probably depends to a large extent on whether you see yourself as a ruler or one who is ruled. Those who don't demonstrate the fruit of the Spirit (no matter how gifted they are) tend to attempt to control others with an iron hand. They see themselves as guides, overseers, or rulers over the people of God. They use their God-given gifts to manipulate others and seek different types of personal and/or corporate gain. Some justify themselves on the grounds that they're not overtly seeking money, but what they don't admit (or perhaps don't even recognize) is that instead they're seeking power and control, which are subtle toxins and even more dangerous.

The ant doesn't have a guide, overseer or ruler. Each ant simply works hard, and God has made them in such a way as to work together without having any need of a controller hierarchy.

Is this not very interesting?

Have you ever seen an ant lying on its back with its legs crossed, having a little nap in the sun?

No!

The ants work night and day. If you damage their house or their path they will soon have it all repaired by the very nature of the life that God has designed them with.

It is true that ants have a queen or queens that regulate to a certain extent the reproduction of the colony, but the ants have no guide, overseer, or ruler that cracks the whip and makes each individual work. Their ability to work hard and in perfect harmony with one another is in their nature.

If we have the life of God, if we've been born again from above by the Spirit of God, if we have the presence of our Lord Jesus in our being, he will cause us to function according to his good pleasure in fellowship and as a team (rather like industrious ants) with others who have the same Spirit, without the need for anyone to be controlling, governing, or obligating us.

He'll place the desire for what he wants us to do right into the depths of our hearts.

> 9 *How long wilt thou sleep, O sluggard?*
> *when wilt thou arise out of thy sleep?*

> 10 *Yet a little sleep, a little slumber, a little*
> *folding of the hands to sleep:*

> 11 *So shall thy poverty come as one that*
> *travels and thy want as an armed man.*

This, of course, is all true at face value in the natural realm. In the spiritual realm, however, many are fast asleep because they have entrusted their spiritual wellbeing to the hands of others, and this is a grave mistake. Clearly, Scripture teaches there is only one mediator between God and man. We must have an ongoing personal relationship with Jesus Christ: he is the only way to the Father.

Entire congregations are filled with those who are spiritually asleep. In the parable of the ten virgins in Matthew 25, both the wise and the foolish are all fast asleep prior to the return of the bridegroom. Such is all too often the case today, when the return of Jesus is at our very door. Even some groups and congregations (symbolized by women in Scripture) that are considered to be wise are still asleep in spiritual lethargy and need to be awakened from their slumber in time to go out and meet the bridegroom as he comes.

Poverty and want may approach as slowly as a weary foot traveler or as unexpectedly as an armed thief breaking into your home. The former was the case with the foolish virgins: minute by minute their lamps used up the supply of oil, and when the virgins woke up, they found that their lights were going out. In the middle of the night, they could not immediately buy oil, and while they sought for a source of the needed fuel, the bridegroom came and the door was shut; they were cut off from the wedding party. "When wilt thou arise from thy sleep?" Too late, alas, too late.

> 12 *A wicked man of Belial walks with a perverse mouth.*
>
> 13 *He winks with his eyes, he speaks with his feet, he teaches with his fingers;*

He winks at evil and leads God's people to believe that they can disobey God and get away with it. His walk is compromised. His fingers point and judge. Such a man is indeed wicked.

> 14 *there is perversion in his heart; he devises evil continually; he sows discord.*
>
> 15 *Therefore his calamity shall come suddenly; suddenly he shall be broken without remedy.*

Such was the fate of Balaam the prophet. At one time, he was in hot demand. Everyone wanted him to prophesy, and his prophecies (at least the ones registered in Scripture) proved to be true. His heart, however, was false, because he sought to use his God-given prophetic gift for personal gain. Therefore, Balaam went down in God's book as a false prophet. Balaam stubbornly refused God's counsel and pleaded to continue his mission, which was allowed. He even prophesied good things about Israel. But his calamity came suddenly when he was killed in the ensuing battle.

The *wicked man of Belial* represents the Devil, even though such a man may be highly gifted and may have mixed in with the people of God. In John 8:42-44, Jesus described a similar scenario:

> *Jesus said unto them, If God were your Father, ye would surely love me, for I proceeded forth and came from God; neither did I come from myself, but he sent me. Why do ye not understand my speech? even because ye cannot hear my word. Ye are of your father the devil, and the desires of your father ye desire to do. He was a murderer from the beginning and abode not in the truth because there is no truth in him. When he speaks a lie, he speaks of his own, for he is a liar and the father of it.*

The Devil was a murderer from the beginning. Does this mean that God created him as a murderer? Hardly. God created everything good, and Satan was part of the initial creation (Genesis 1:31). But he was a murderer from the beginning of his rebellion. Satan founded the evil system of this world when he came against Adam and Eve with lies and deception until he was able to usurp their God-given authority over creation. In order to bring about the division between Adam and God, he had to twist the truth and introduce murder and death.

16 *These six things does the LORD hate:*
yea, seven are an abomination unto him:

17 *A proud look, a lying tongue, and*
hands that shed innocent blood,

18 *a heart that devises wicked imagina-*
tions, feet that are swift in running to evil,

19 *a false witness that speaks lies, and he*
that sows discord among brethren.

This is a basic description of the natural, fallen man without God. It's also a description of what happens when the natural, fallen man is in charge of what are supposed to be the people of God. This applies not only to the religious leaders of Jesus' day but to vast numbers of church leaders ever since and has been getting worse and worse over time because once corruption sets in, it will always get worse. For this reason God is once again about to take radical action, as he did in the days of Noah. *But as the days of Noah were, so shall also the coming of the Son of man be* (Matthew 24:37).

What exactly was going on in the days of Noah? According to Genesis 6:5-8:

And GOD saw that the wickedness of
man was great in the earth and that every
imagination of the thoughts of his heart
was only evil continually. And the LORD
repented of having made man on the
earth, and it grieved him at his heart. And
the LORD said, I will destroy man whom
I have created from the face of the earth,

both man and beast and the animals and the fowls of the air, for I repent of having made them. But Noah found grace in the eyes of the LORD.

The book of Proverbs illustrates more about grace.

20 My son, keep thy father's commandment and forsake not the law of thy mother:

21 Bind them continually upon thine heart and tie them about thy neck.

22 When thou goest, it shall lead thee; when thou sleepest, it shall keep thee; and when thou awakest, it shall talk with thee.

Noah means rest. Noah stopped and began to listen to God, and he found grace in the eyes of the Lord. The rest of the ancient world continued on their merry way – right into perdition.

If God is our Father, if we've been born again from above by the Spirit, God will speak in and through our hearts; we can only hear his still, small voice as we make hearing and obeying him our top priority. If we're born from above, then the *Jerusalem from above* is our mother. If all of those who are born-again citizens of the heavenly Jerusalem are our *mother*, then what is *the law of our mother*? Jesus only gave us one new law or commandment: that we should love one another even as he has loved us. Jesus gave his life for us; we should be willing to give our lives for our brethren (John 3:16; 1 John 3:16).

23 For the commandment is fire, and the

> *law is light; and reproofs of chastening are*
> *the way of life,*

Hearing directly from God the Father is a fire that will cleanse the very depths of our being. The law of love that flows through all of the people of God who have been born from above by the Spirit is light. Jesus said, *Ye are the light of the world* (Matthew 5:14). The reproofs of chastening that we receive by the Spirit of God are what keep us centered on the way of life instead of the way of death, which is the course of the natural, fallen man.

But why is all of this needed? Why is it necessary for the Lord to guide our every step?

Why isn't it sufficient to read a chapter from the Bible every morning, say a short prayer, and make sure we're in church each Sunday morning?

Why isn't it enough to simply pay our tithe into the church treasury and spend the rest of our money any fool way we please?

Why is it necessary to be guided when we walk, when we sleep, when we're awake?

Why must the commandment of God the Father be fire?

> 24 *to keep thee from the evil woman,*
> *from the flattery of the tongue of a strange*
> *woman.*

This key advice is not confined to the natural realm. After all, in the earthly world, fallen men can easily be seduced by an attractive stranger, but what about godly women – do they also need to be kept from this evil, strange, smooth-tongued woman? Yes indeed, because spiritually, a strange woman is a symbol of a congregation that is not in tune with God, a congregation where Jesus has withdrawn the lampstand of his presence (Revelation 2:5).

The Scripture is for everyone: men, women, and children.

> 25 *Lust not after her beauty in thine heart,*
> *neither let her take thee with her eyes.*

The structure of the building may be magnificent. The choir and orchestra may be sublime. Facilities for children and young people of all ages may be expansive. But the meetings may be performance-oriented instead of Spirit-led; the missions and outreach programs may be project-focused instead of people-oriented. Courses and procedures and training may capacitate everyone, molding them as a brick factory of Babylon or Egypt, instead of allowing the Lord to individually sculpt each living stone. The family unit (which God has set as the nucleus for society) may be separated, with each member of the family in a different program or class. The stranger's outward beauty is stunning and her eyes mesmerizing. But what lies behind that façade may be another matter altogether.

> 26 *For by means of a whorish woman a*
> *man is reduced to a piece of bread, and*
> *the woman will hunt the precious soul of*
> *the man.*

What happened with Adam? Why did he fall? Why did he literally lose his soul? Why, when God had initially set him over everything, was he reduced to tilling the soil by the sweat of his brow for a piece of bread?

He was unable to break the soul tie with Eve.

He listened to the deceived woman instead of to God. After she believed the lie of the enemy, she thought that the fruit of the tree of the knowledge of good and evil would make them as wise as God, so she tasted the forbidden fruit.

This is still the root of the problem behind the deception of strange women (as individuals or as corporate congregations or religious organizations).

Along the road of life, I've experienced a few unhealthy relationships myself, but by the grace of God, I've been able to escape from them or break them off. The Holy Spirit has never allowed me to enter into binding horizontal relationships with individuals, groups, churches, missions, or any other entity that might supersede or interfere in any way with my commitment to the Lord. My commitment to God is my top priority, and because of my exclusive relationship with him, I'm led by the Holy Spirit into loving fellowship with so many others who have the same Spirit and commitment. What holds the true body of Christ together is our commitment to Jesus, the head, and to the Father, not horizontal commitments to one another or to institutions or programs.

> 27 *Can a man take fire in his bosom and*
> *his clothes not be burned?*

Our clothes are our covering by obedience to the Spirit of God. If we embrace the wrong woman in either the natural realm or the spiritual, the consequences will be devastating. Our true covering will go up in smoke.

> 28 *Can one go upon hot coals, and his feet not be burned?*

> 29 *So is he that goes in to his neighbor's wife; whosoever touches her shall not be innocent.*

> 30 *Men do not take a thief lightly, even if he steals to satisfy his soul when he is hungry;*

> 31 *and once he is taken, he shall restore sevenfold; he shall give all the substance of his house.*

> 32 *But whosoever commits adultery with a woman has a fault in his heart; he that does it corrupts his own soul.*

Remember that David is writing this after his affair with Bathsheba that almost brought down his kingdom. It's curious to note that after David was restored and forgiven, God even let Bathsheba remain with him (she had nowhere else to go after David had instigated the murder of her husband, Uriah), and Solomon was the son of the union of David with Bathsheba after their first child died. Nevertheless, the consequences of David's sin were very severe: he was banished from his kingdom for several months by Absalom, his son, and ended up losing a total of four sons.

> 33 *A wound and dishonour shall he get, and his reproach shall never be wiped away.*

34 For the jealous rage of a man will not spare in the day of vengeance.

35 He will not regard any ransom; neither will he want to forgive, though thou givest many bribes.

After Bathsheba became pregnant from the adulterous relationship with David, the situation got even more complicated because it became impossible for David to deal with her husband, Uriah. This, in turn, led to Uriah's murder.

Rest assured that any improper soul tie with a *strange woman* is a certain recipe for downfall. Adultery is deadly in the natural and in the spiritual, but only the direct correction, discipline, and chastening of God can prevent us from yielding to it (or correct the situation, such as in the case of David).

Here is a final thought:

God has a people of whom he is very jealous. Those who run around claiming to be in the "husband" ministry, saying that they are the spiritual husband of a given congregation (or congregations), could wind up in a lot of trouble on the *day of vengeance.*

Those who attempt to control the people of God are greatly mistaken, and in the day of the return of the Lord, they will find themselves in a serious and insoluble problem. How would you like to face the glorious, resurrected Jesus Christ, who now has all power and all authority, while you're under the charge of having made indecent advances to his wife?

If we turn this around, Satan also has a people upon

the earth. There is a great harlot described in Revelation, who has many daughters. There is also the example of Jezebel and her sons and daughters and false prophets. Whoever is caught fooling around with the wife or the daughters of the Devil will also be in terrible trouble in the day of the Lord.

Let Us Pray:

Heavenly Father, we ask that we may have clarity over these words and clarity over those with whom we should associate. May we be united only with those who walk in your paths. May we discern and appreciate the wife of our youth; our calling; and our place in God related to the true body of Christ.

May we receive our sustenance from the right source and not from the wrong one. May we see things as they really are and not find ourselves embracing an abomination. May we be sensitive to the Holy Spirit and quick to seek correction and cleansing if we have offended your Spirit.

Deliver us from making commitments and covenants that you do not approve of; deliver us from relationships or soul ties with persons or groups that will compete with our relationship with you.

If we are in a trap with a rope around our neck, please allow us to escape before it is too late.

We ask this in the name of our Lord Jesus Christ. Amen.

Chapter 7

Hearken Unto Chastening, and Be Wise

Proverbs 7

1 *My son, keep my words, and lay up my commandments with thee.*

2 *Keep my commandments, and live; and my law as the apple of thine eye.*

3 *Bind them upon thy fingers; write them upon the tablet of thine heart.*

4 *Say unto wisdom, Thou art my sister, and call understanding thy kinswoman:*

5 *That they may keep thee from the woman belonging to someone else, from the stranger who flatters with her words.*

This is speaking of God's law, which is in a certain sense personified. We must take into account that this is in the Old Testament and we are now in the New Testament; but the Old Testament is full of examples and foreshadowings that become reality in the New Testament.

The Lord Jesus fulfilled the law and taught in this manner. He said:

> *Ye have heard that it was said to the ancients, Thou shalt not commit murder, and whosoever shall commit murder shall be guilty of the judgment; but I say unto you, That whosoever is angry with his brother out of control shall be in danger of the judgment* (Matthew 5:21-22).

On the same occasion, he taught:

> *Ye have heard that it was said to the ancients, Thou shalt not commit adultery; but I say unto you, That whosoever looks on a woman to lust after her has committed adultery with her already in his heart* (Matthew 5:27-28).

In the New Covenant, we're not under the law if we are the sons of God being led by the Spirit of God, but that doesn't mean the law of God does not apply: it means that we're being held to an even higher standard, which has to do with the attitude and status of our hearts.

Throughout his life, Solomon had many women. He sought alliances with other kingdoms and married hundreds of daughters of pagan kings. The pagan women turned the heart of Solomon away from God and towards their pagan gods until great damage was done to Israel, the people of God.

Solomon became a very striking example of what would transpire during the age in which there would be many churches (women). He began by building the temple of God and then built pagan temples and shrines, which lasted for hundreds of years, all over the high places of Israel. Some of the effects of Solomon's apostasy have stained Israel even unto now.

> 6 *For at the window of my house I looked through my casement*
>
> 7 *and beheld among the simple ones, I discerned among the youths, a young man void of understanding,*
>
> 8 *passing through the street near her corner; and he went the way to her house,*
>
> 9 *in the twilight, in the evening, in the black and dark night.*

In the natural realm, the consequences of adultery are extremely serious and leave an indelible mark upon the soul. Spiritual adultery is even more serious. Those who join their soul to the wrong group or congregation are like the person that frequents the house of the strange woman. The path to her house leads into the twilight of the evening and the black and dark night.

And now more than ever, if we are at the end of the day of man and the end of the age of the church, spiritually speaking, is it day or is it night?

Night surrounds us as we await the dawning of the new day of the Lord; now is when the black and dark night is most intense. We are not in the time of

Renaissance or Reformation. We are not in the time of the Great Awakening. No! We are in the prophesied time when the love of many has grown cold (Matthew 24:12). We are in the time when there is a famine of hearing the words of the Lord.

With a flurry of religious activity, many are seeking signs and wonders, and great multitudes are being congregated, but the charity (the love of God) of many has waxed cold. This is a key time for our hearts to remain focused, because those who endure unto the end shall be saved (Matthew 24:13).

This book of Proverbs is not primarily an intellectual book. It deals with matters of the heart, and the model is the heart of God. True wisdom, understanding, and intelligence flow from God's heart. Our hearts must be submitted and joined to his in order for the knowledge of God to flow into our minds. Unless our hearts are right, our human intellectual capacity will lead us into twilight and into the black and dark night of our own fantasies and illusions.

> 10 *and, behold, a woman met him with the attire of a harlot, and subtil of heart.*
>
> 11 *(She is loud and stubborn; her feet do not abide in her house:*
>
> 12 *Now without, now in the streets, she lies in wait at every corner.)*

Almost everywhere, the true love and fire of God has diminished or gone out. Those who are seeking the strange woman of the corrupt and contaminated religious houses of prostitution are in more and more danger. As the night gets darker and blacker, they have less and less discernment, and she seems more and more attractive.

We are now at the time of the harvest, and God is seeking to bring his people to maturity in Christ; he is seeking to perfect their walk. Those who, at the end of the growing season, are still immature young men (regardless of their sex or age) are easy prey for the harlot system as they wander to and fro seeking the latest sensational (or even supernatural) religious fad.

> 13 *So she caught him and kissed him and with an impudent face said unto him,*
>
> 14 *I had promised sacrifices of peace; today I have payed my vows.*
>
> 15 *Therefore I came forth to meet thee, diligently to seek thy face, and I have found thee.*

Her language is religious and seemingly pious. She sounds as though she is speaking of total commitment to God. She says that this is the reason she has come forth to meet him. She makes it sound as if it is a divine act of providence that she has found him.

> 16 *I have decked my bed with coverings of tapestry, with carved works, with fine linen of Egypt.*

Her sumptuous sanctuaries are decked with tapestries covered with slogans. The pulpit and the altar are made of meticulously carved works full of religious symbols. The fine linen of Egypt is extended over the communion table. You have probably been there on more than one occasion, you know the place. To anyone with real godly discernment, it reeks of human horizontal covering and the dead works of self-righteousness. Egypt typifies this with the strong human control of modern-day Pharaohs. Her bed is decked with the trappings of religious legalism while at the same time, her life style is promiscuous.

> 17 *I have perfumed my bed with myrrh,*
> *aloes, and cinnamon.*

Myrrh can be a symbol of the cross, aloes of health, and cinnamon of righteousness. She sounds very anointed, but she's lying. Even though her sanctuaries and architecture are filled with prominent displays of the cross (she may even hang one around her neck), she knows nothing of the real way of the cross that will bring about the death of the old man. Her aloes aren't saving anyone's health. They are superficial or emotional religious experiences that will save no one. Her cinnamon is really self-righteousness and is an abomination to the Lord.

> 18 *Come, let us take our fill of love until*
> *the morning; let us solace ourselves with*
> *loves.*

The messages from her pulpit emphasize gooey horizontal human love. Words like *repentance*, *judgment*, and *holiness* are like a foreign language to her. She knows nothing of the true agape love of God that is born of sacrifice and redemptive by its very nature. She knows nothing of the correction, discipline, and chastening of Father God. She promises that the black and dark night will turn into morning while she embraces those who are naïve and immature and lulls them to sleep, oblivious of their real danger.

> 19 *For the husband is not home; he is gone a long journey:*
>
> 20 *He has taken a bag of money with him and will come home at the appointed feast day.*

Even though she claims that Jesus is her husband, he has gone away on a long journey (almost two thousand years ago). She knows that he will come back at the appointed time, but she has no fear of the Lord. She thinks that Jesus paid it all (with a big bag of money) and that we don't have to worry about walking circumspectly in holiness.

> 21 *With her much fair speech she caused him to yield; with the flattering of her lips she persuaded him.*
>
> 22 *He went after her straightway, as an ox goes to the slaughter or as a fool to the correction of the stocks,*
>
> 23 *until the arrow pierces through his liver. He is as a bird struggling in the snare and not knowing that it is against his own life.*

What is the function of the liver? It is to purify the blood, and the life is in the blood (Leviticus 17:11). The liver is equivalent to the conscience. Once the strange woman has placed her arrow through his liver, he's done. It's over. He cannot escape her trap.

She knows exactly how to manage guilt and ensnare the person so they can never be free. In her house there is no victory over sin, only endless cycles of sin and guilt and religious activity. Many go to her confessional or to her counseling services and blindly submit to her spiritual directors.

> 24 *Hearken unto me now therefore, O ye sons, and attend to the words of my mouth.*
>
> 25 *Let not thine heart decline to her ways; do not go astray in her paths.*
>
> 26 *For she has caused many to fall down dead; yea, all the strong men have been slain by her.*
>
> 27 *Her house is the way to Sheol, going down to the chambers of death.*

If this was just a simple story about carnal seduction, it wouldn't say that *all the strong* have been slain by her. All of those who are strong in their own strength to fulfill religious ritual and exercise, all who are strong in their own self-righteousness will have their spiritual discernment extinguished when she lulls them to sleep in her bed and pierces through their liver with her arrow. This is primarily speaking of spiritual death (such as what happened to Adam and Eve on the very day that they touched the forbidden fruit).

Proverbs 8

*1 Doth not wisdom cry, and give her voice
to intelligence?*

Wisdom cries and gives her voice to intelligence by the Spirit of God through the true people of God, of which Jesus is the first and the last (Revelation 1:11). *Wisdom*, in Hebrew, is of feminine gender even though it is identical to Jesus Christ. This is because Jesus is the first of the firstfruits of a new creation. In that which has already been created, nothing was done without him (Colossians 1:12-20). The same also applies to the new creation.

Jesus, the head of the body, is male, but the first-fruits (the sum of all the members of the body) are female even though the individual sons (both men and women, regardless of gender) are referred to in the male gender. The nation of the people of God is referred to as a woman in prophetic terminology. God looks at the potential of the seed; and Jesus is the seed that fell into the ground and died so his life could be multiplied into people like us.

Therefore, the wisdom that is begotten of God, before the creation of the heavens and the earth, is a seed that God wants to multiply into an entire nation that will flow with his wisdom and understanding (Isaiah 66:8).

*2 She stands in the top of high places, by
the way at the crossroads of the paths.*

*3 She cries at the gates, at the entry of the
city, at the coming in at the doors.*

The true people of God are a clean woman (and Jesus is the head). She has a clean message. God desires for the witness of his people to be put on display, showing the way back to God. This is wisdom.

> 4 *Unto you, O men, I call; and my voice is to the sons of men.*

This reference to sons of men, even though it seems to be in the masculine gender, is referring to both men and women. The same is true of the term *sons of God*.

What does wisdom desire?

That the sons of men become sons of God and come to maturity under the correction and chastening of the Father. Now she tells us in plain language:

> 5 *O ye simple, understand prudence; and ye fools, be ye of an understanding heart.*

> 6 *Hear, for I will speak of excellent things, and the opening of my lips shall be right things.*

> 7 *For my mouth shall speak truth, and wickedness is an abomination to my lips.*

> 8 *All the words of my mouth are in righteousness; there is nothing perverse or twisted in them.*

> 9 *They are all plain to him that understands and right to those that have found wisdom.*

> 10 *Receive my chastening and not silver, and knowledge rather than choice gold.*

11 *For wisdom is better than precious stones; and all the things that may be desired are not to be compared to it.*

12 *I, wisdom, dwell with prudence, and I invent the knowledge of giving counsel.*

13 *The fear of the LORD is to hate evil; pride, arrogancy, the evil way, and the perverse mouth, do I hate.*

14 *With me is counsel, and existence; I am understanding; strength belongs to me.*

Counsel and existence are in the eternal life of the Lord. We cannot guarantee our own existence, let alone give wise counsel. God the Father can truly say *I AM*, and so can Jesus Christ, his only begotten Son, who is our strength. If we have Jesus, we have life; if we don't have Jesus, we don't have life (1 John 5:11-12). It's that simple.

15 *By me the kings reign, and the princes decree justice.*

16 *By me the princes rule, and all of the governors judge the earth.*

17 *I love those that love me, and those that seek me early shall find me.*

This is definitely not out of our reach.

18 *Riches and honour are with me, yea, durable riches and righteousness.*

19 *My fruit is better than gold, yea, than*

*precious stones, and my revenue than
choice silver.*

20 *I shall lead in the way of righteousness
in the midst of the paths of judgment,*

21 *that I may cause my friends to inherit
existence and I will fill their treasures.*

Jesus said that those who keep his commandments
are his friends and he will share his intimate plans and
secrets with his friends (John 15:14-15).

22 *The LORD possessed me in the beginning of his way, before his works of old.*

23 *I was set up with eternal dominion,
from the beginning, before the earth was.*

24 *I was begotten before the depths, before
the existence of the fountains of many
waters.*

Scripture states that Jesus Christ is the only begotten Son of God (John 3:16). He is also called the Word
(John 1:1). Here his name is Wisdom, and he obviously
predates Genesis 1:1. As he tells us in words of poetic
beauty:

25 *Before the mountains were founded,
before the hills was I begotten.*

26 *While as yet he had not made the earth
nor the fields nor the beginning of the dust
of the world,*

27 *when he composed the heavens, I was*

there. When he set a compass upon the face of the depth,

28 *when he established the clouds above, when he strengthened the fountains of the deep,*

29 *when he gave to the sea his decree that the waters should not pass his commandment, when he appointed the foundations of the earth,*

30 *I was with him ordering everything; I was his delight every day, being content before him at all times;*

31 *I am content in the circumference of his earth, and my contentment is with the sons of men.*

32 *Now therefore hearken unto me, O ye sons; for blessed are those that keep my ways.*

33 *Hearken unto chastening, and be wise; refuse it not.*

34 *Blessed is the man that hears me, keeping vigil at my gates, waiting at the threshold of my doors.*

35 *For whosoever finds me shall find life and shall obtain the will of the LORD.*

36 *But he that sins against me wrongs*

*his own soul; all those that hate me love
death.*

Therefore, we must make good use of the time that
has been given us upon this earth and live each day as
if it were our last day here, in the midst of this corrupt
and fallen world, where we have the opportunity to
find wisdom and to grow in grace and in favor before
God and before men.

Let Us Pray:

*Heavenly Father, may this message become reality in us.
May we submit to your advice, correction and chastening
so that we do not fall into the arms of the wrong woman
at this most critical hour.*

*We ask this in the name of our Lord Jesus Christ.
Amen.*

Chapter 8

The Lips of the Righteous Shall Know the Will of God

Proverbs 9

The number *nine* is an interesting number in Scripture. It's three multiplied by three, which in mathematical language is three squared. Three refers to life and planting, growing, and harvesting. When the number is squared, the consequences of those factors relating to spiritual results are metaphorically squared too.

Therefore, as nine reflects the square of three, the planting, growing, and harvesting reflect the ultimate harvesting, the final judgment. The consequences of that judgment may be good or bad depending upon what was planted, how it was cultivated, and what was harvested.

> 1 *Wisdom has built her house; she has hewn out her seven pillars:*

2 *She has killed her sacrifice; she has mingled her wine; and she has furnished her table.*

3 *She has sent forth her maidens; she cries upon the highest places of the city,*

4 *whosoever is simple, let him turn in here; as for those that lack understanding, she saith unto him,*

5 *Come, eat of my bread, and drink of the wine which I have mingled.*

6 *Forsake that which is foolish and live and go in the way of understanding.*

Wisdom is personified in Proverbs. When she has built her house, she invites people to a banquet. The Scriptures mention several such invitations. They also state that we are the temple that God is building and that when he is finished (*seven pillars* means that all the pillars are in place), he will put this house built of living stones on display for the entire world to see.

Two elements that are necessary in order to make a covenant are bread and wine. The first mention of this was when Abraham, returning from the slaughter of the kings, was blessed by Melchizedek, king of Salem, who *brought forth bread and wine, for he was the priest of the most high God* (Genesis 14:18).

In verse 2, the sacrifice that must be killed is the way and desires of the flesh; the wine that she serves is the life of Christ; and the bread with which she has furnished her table is the body of Christ, broken for us. Though the body of Christ has been mistreated and broken throughout all these long centuries, we can still be fed and nurtured by it, just as we may still sip from the wine of his life. This is wisdom.

> 7 *He that chastens a scorner brings shame unto himself, and he that chastens a wicked man brings himself a blot.*

> 8 *Chasten not a scorner lest he hate thee; chasten a wise man, and he will love thee.*

> 9 *Give instruction to a wise man, and he will be yet wiser; teach a just man, and he will increase in learning.*

In the natural realm, we can see that those young people who have a bad attitude toward their teachers will not be able to learn certain things. Obviously, we have even worse impediments in the educational system now that many of those scorners have become teachers and professors, which makes it even more difficult for any real correction to take place. If the professor, the human teacher, is unjust, cynical, contaminated, and without a moral compass, it's no wonder the young people either don't learn well or learn those things which are not convenient, bringing *shame* and *a blot* upon society.

> 10 *The fear of the LORD is the beginning of wisdom, and the knowledge of the holy is understanding.*

Wisdom begins with a proper respect for the Lord, and the knowledge of the holy is the importance of being separated for his exclusive use. Those who understand this live to make God happy, and we can know this through our conscience. We live so God, by the Holy Spirit, can work in us and through us. This is the path to true satisfaction.

Holiness is not a certain religious manner of acting or speaking, nor is it conforming to a list of dos and don'ts. *The kingdom of God is not food or drink, but righteousness and peace and joy in the Holy Spirit* (Romans 14:17).

Those who claim that they cannot hear the voice of God can begin by listening to their own conscience in the fear of the Lord.

> 11 *For by me thy days shall be multiplied,*
> *and the years of thy life shall be increased.*

> 12 *If thou be wise, thou shalt be wise for*
> *thyself; but if thou scornest, thou alone*
> *shall bear it.*

Wisdom that comes from hearing the voice of the Lord will lead us to eternal life. This is not our own natural life continuing into infinity but an entirely different quality of life that brings us into the inner peace of knowing that we are pleasing God. Eternal life is God's life.

There are only two possible paths. The way of wisdom leads to eternal life, and the way of the scorner leads to death. Each path has its consequences, and the number *nine* is a scriptural signifier of the weightiness of those consequences: life or death.

13 *A foolish woman is clamorous: she is simple and knows nothing.*

14 *For she sits at the door of her house on a seat in the high places of the city*

15 *to call to those who pass by the way, to those who straighten their ways;*

16 *Whosoever is simple, let him turn in here; and as for him that lacks understanding, she saith unto him:*

17 *Stolen waters are sweet, and bread eaten in secret is pleasant.*

18 *But he does not know that the dead are there and that her guests are in the depths of Sheol.*

Two women are being contrasted in this chapter. One is wise and the other is foolish. One represents the clean people of God, and the other represents the lost people of the Devil. The foolish woman has a seat in the high places of the city. She commits fornication with the kings of the earth. She operates within the synagogues, congregations, churches, and religious organizations that are her house. Right now the wheat (the sons of God) and the tares (the sons of the evil one) are still growing together in the same field, but at the time of the harvest, the judgment will commence, and the tares will be taken out and burned. When this happens, we want to be a safe distance away from the tares. Thus, as we rapidly approach the time of the end, it is paramount that we not be found in the embrace of the wrong woman.

Compare the scenes described in the following Scriptures and notice that the order of events is the same as that of the wheat and the tares.

The first is Matthew 13:40-43:

> *As therefore the tares are gathered and burned in the fire, so shall it be in the end of this age. The Son of man shall send forth his angels, and they shall gather out of his kingdom all things that offend and those who do iniquity and shall cast them into the furnace of fire; there shall be wailing and gnashing of teeth. Then shall the righteous shine forth as the sun in the kingdom of their Father. He who has ears to hear, let him hear.*

Revelation 18:3-8 tends to focus primarily on the fate of the tares:

> *For all the Gentiles have drunk of the wine of the wrath of her fornication, and the kings of the earth have committed forni-cation with her, and the merchants of the earth are waxed rich through the power of her delicacies. And I heard another voice from the heaven, saying, Come out of her, my people, that ye not be partakers of her sins, and that ye receive not of her plagues. For her sins have reached unto the heaven, and God has remembered*

her iniquities. Reward her even as she rewarded you and pay her double according to her works; in the cup which she has given thee to drink, give her double. As much as she has glorified herself and lived deliciously, give her that much torment and sorrow; for she says in her heart, I sit a queen, and am no widow, and shall see no sorrow. Therefore, shall her plagues come in one day, death and mourning and famine; and she shall be utterly burned with fire; for strong is the Lord God who judges her.

Revelation 19:7-9, on the other hand, describes the joy that awaits the wheat:

Let us be glad and rejoice and give glory to him; for the marriage of the Lamb is come, and his bride has made herself ready. And to her was granted that she should be arrayed in fine linen, clean and bright: for the fine linen is the righteousness of the saints. And he said unto me, Write, Blessed are those who are called unto the marriage supper of the Lamb. And he said unto me, These are the true words of God.

Let us Pray:

Heavenly Father, may your hand continually be upon us. May we be delivered from the snare of the strange woman. May we always be satisfied and content with your provision for us. We ask this in the name of our Lord Jesus Christ. Amen.

Chapter 9

The Parables of Solomon

The following chapters contain proverbs or parables that Solomon gleaned and compiled during the golden age of Israel. Many relate prophetically to the coming day of the Lord, which will usher in the real Golden Age at the second coming of Jesus Christ.

Parables are true at face value but also have a much deeper meaning that must be properly interpreted. The face value makes a certain amount of sense to the natural man, but only God can give the spiritual interpretation. Jesus taught by parables that even the religious authorities of his day could not interpret.

For example, any farmer can understand the face value of the parable of the wheat and the tares. In the interpretation he gave to his disciples, however, Jesus explained that the field is the world, the good seed are the sons of the kingdom, and the tares are the sons of the wicked (Matthew 13:36-43).

Here are the proverbs and parables of Proverbs 10:

Proverbs 10

1 A wise son makes a glad father; but a foolish son is sadness unto his mother.

The wise son is led by the Spirit. The foolish son goes the way of the strange woman.

2 Treasures of wickedness profit nothing, but righteousness delivers from death.

3 The LORD will not suffer the soul of the righteous to famish, but wickedness shall cast out the wicked.

What is righteousness? It's being what God wants us to be so that we can do what he wants us to do. We're very close to an end-time prophetic fulfillment of this parable. The wicked are about to be removed from among the righteous. Wickedness shall cast them out! Many teachers have twisted this the other way around, claiming that the righteous are about to be raptured while the wicked will remain, but this verse tells us plainly that that won't be the case.

4 He that deals with a slack hand becomes poor, but the hand of the diligent makes rich.

Many are teaching that because Jesus paid it all, there's nothing left for us to do, but the truth is we are to be faithful with whatever talent or responsibility Jesus has given us until he returns (Matthew 25:14-30).

5 He that gathers in summer is a wise son, but he that sleeps in harvest is a son that causes shame.

Paul wrote to Timothy that he should be instant in

preaching the word, both in season and out of season (2 Timothy 4:2). Many think that it is not the right time to be busy in the work of the harvest. It's a shame and a blot that so many are spiritually asleep right when there are so many opportunities for the kingdom.

> 6 *Blessings are upon the head of the just, but the mouth of the wicked covers violence.*
>
> 7 *The memory of the just is blessed, but the name of the wicked shall stink.*
>
> 8 *The wise in heart will receive the commandments, but he who speaks foolishly shall fall.*

The wise will receive personalized commandments from God 24/7, 365 days/year – that's how much our Father God loves us and wants to guide us in the right path.

> 9 *He that walks with integrity walks securely, but he that perverts his ways shall be broken.*
>
> 10 *He that winks with the eye causes sorrow, and he that speaks foolishness shall fall.*
>
> 11 *The mouth of a righteous man is a well of life, but the mouth of the wicked covers violence.*
>
> 12 *Hatred stirs up strifes, but love covers all sins.*

The one who has hatred in his heart stirs up more

and more resentment when he speaks in public and even in private. The one who loves will cover for his friends and may even speak in as positive a manner as possible regarding his enemies. As followers of Christ, we overcome evil with good (Romans 12:21).

> 13 *In the lips of the prudent wisdom is found and is a rod unto the back of him that is void of understanding.*

The prudent don't respond in the heat of the moment: they wait until God moves them. And if God doesn't move them, they neither speak nor act. Prudence has to do not only with our words but also with our actions; it should be a major factor in how we go about doing things.

> 14 *Wise men keep knowledge, but the mouth of the foolish is near unto calamity.*

> 15 *The rich man's wealth is his strong city; the weakness of the poor is their poverty.*

We are to be rich in wisdom and understanding by the blessing of the Lord.

The meaning of a number of the verses is self-evident:

> 16 *The work of the righteous is unto life, but the fruit of the wicked is for sin.*

> 17 *He is in the way of life that gives heed to chastening, but he that refuses reproof errs.*

> 18 *He that hides hatred has lying lips, and he that utters a slander, is a fool.*

> 19 *In the multitude of words there is no*

lack of rebellion, but he that refrains his lips is wise.

20 The tongue of the just is as choice silver, but the understanding of the wicked is worth little.

21 The lips of the righteous feed many, but fools die for lack of wisdom.

22 The blessing of the LORD is that which makes rich, and he adds no sorrow with it.

23 To make an abomination is as sport to the fool, but wisdom is recreation to the man of intelligence.

An abomination excludes the presence of the Lord; wisdom flows from God's presence.

24 The fear of the wicked, it shall come upon him, but God shall grant the desire of the righteous.

25 When the whirlwind passes, the wicked is no more, but the righteous is founded for ever.

26 As vinegar to the teeth and as smoke to the eyes, so is the sluggard to those that send him.

27 The fear of the LORD shall prolong days, but the years of the wicked shall be shortened.

28 The hope of the righteous is joy, but the hope of the wicked shall perish.

> 29 *The way of the LORD is strength to the*
> *perfect, but it is terror to the workers of*
> *iniquity.*

The word *perfect* is the same as *mature* in Hebrew. The houses of religion that belong to the strange woman teach that it's impossible for any of us to be perfect. They maintain their people in a perpetual state of immaturity by impeding them from being dealt with directly by God. In the true plan of God, it's imperative that we come to maturity in Christ if we are to stand fast in the tribulation and judgment that is about to come upon the face of the earth. There are many religious people who are terrified of what God is about to do as he brings this age to a close.

Jesus said, *Be ye therefore perfect, even as your Father who is in the heavens is perfect* (Matthew 5:48). He would not have given us this order if it weren't possible for us to follow it. In the fallen nature of Adam, no one will ever be perfect, but in Christ all things are possible. If we submit to the chastening of God, he will correct us and grant us grace so that we will come to maturity in Christ. He promises not only to forgive our sins but to cleanse us from all unrighteousness (1 John 1:9). This is the place of victory!

> 30 *The righteous eternally shall never be*
> *removed, but the wicked shall not inhabit*
> *the earth.*

The prophetic component of these proverbs (or parables) is undeniable. The present age has persecuted, reviled, slandered, tortured, and killed untold millions of righteous persons (Matthew 5:10-12). There is more persecution now than ever. Yet God promises to bring all these righteous persons back in a first resurrection, when they shall reign with Christ for a thousand years (Revelation 20:4).

The prophecy teachers for millions of Christians believe and teach that there will be a secret rapture – that God will remove all of the Christians to heaven (including so-called carnal or lukewarm Christians). They also teach that God will remove the Holy Spirit from the earth, and wickedness will completely dominate for a certain period of time (some say three-and-a-half years, some say seven years, and now some are even saying seventy years). But God says plainly that the righteous shall never be removed. It is the wicked who will be cut off and removed from among the righteous.

> 31 *The mouth of the just shall bring forth wisdom, but the perverse tongue shall be cut off.*

Notice that this is in the future tense. The time will soon come when all those who are speaking perversion will be cut off.

> 32 *The lips of the righteous shall know the will of God, but the mouth of the wicked speaks perversion.*

Let Us Pray:

Heavenly Father, may we be among those who rejoice at your timely correction so that our lips may know your will. We ask this in the name of our Lord Jesus. Amen.

Chapter 10

The House of the Righteous Shall Remain

Proverbs 11

1 A false balance is an abomination to the LORD, but a just weight is his delight.

There are those who buy with one weight or measure and sell with another. When the balance is altered and transactions become dishonest, the presence of the Lord leaves. Yet if we look at the monetary systems of the world, virtually all of them are based on a false balance. Paper money that is printed as deemed necessary, without being backed by anything of real and constant value, tends to cause inflation as the money devalues. Anyone with savings loses money while whoever controls the printing presses gains it. Similar things happen in the spiritual realm, as religious institutions churn out self-righteous graduates (decked out with certificates) who may not have been converted from the heart.

2 *When pride comes, then comes shame,*
but with the humble is wisdom.

The sin of Satan had its origin in a heady dose of pride. He desired to magnify himself because he couldn't accept that God had given Adam authority over the garden of God. The consequences of listening to Satan left Adam and Eve ashamed and naked, whereas if they had humbly submitted to the will of God, they would have found the tree of life.

3 *The perfection of the upright shall guide*
them in the way, but the perverseness of
transgressors shall destroy them.

Remember that *perfection* is the same word as *maturity*. Jesus Christ is perfect and mature, and he desires to reign and rule from our hearts. In Scripture, the first part of our being that is linked with the possibility of perfection is our hearts. Even in the Old Testament, there are many examples of those who, according to God, had a perfect heart to follow him (2 Kings 20:3; 1 Chronicles 12:38; 1 Chronicles 29:9).

Many teach that in our human condition, we cannot aspire to perfection. This is due, in part, to the fact that our modern language has redefined the word so that in popular use it no longer retains its original meaning. Fruit that has come to maturity (perfection) in the biblical sense simply means fruit that is now useful for food and for seed, even though there might be a little blemish or deformity here or there. A perfect grain of wheat is one, which after being planted, will reproduce and multiply according to its nature.

Even though we may never score a hundred percent on every math test (or any math test) due to our human condition, it's possible for us to live with our hearts set one hundred percent on following the Lord and receiving the correction, chastening, and blessing of our heavenly Father. It's possible for us to live with a clean conscience before God. This is the true meaning of the word *perfection* in Scripture.

> 4 *Riches shall not profit in the day of wrath, but righteousness shall deliver from death.*

This is obviously prophetic. The day of wrath is not very far off. Those who are self-righteous are fooling themselves.

> 5 *The righteousness of the perfect shall straighten his way, but the wicked shall fall by his own wickedness.*

Righteousness and perfection are linked. Jesus Christ is perfect, and we may walk in his righteousness instead of in our own self-righteousness. The personification of wickedness is the Devil, who also has a very large family of those who follow in his footsteps. Jesus described them as tares planted among the wheat.

> 6 *The righteousness of the upright shall deliver them, but transgressors shall be imprisoned in their own sin.*

Those who knowingly go against the will of the Lord become imprisoned and trapped by their own sin, and only Jesus can deliver them. Those who cross a certain line, thinking that they can come back whenever they wish, are deluding themselves. Even the Devil will soon be imprisoned in Hades for a thousand years, along with the souls of many others who have been there over the past six thousand years, awaiting final judgment (Revelation 20:1-3).

> 7 *When the wicked man dies, his hope perishes, and the hope of unjust men shall perish.*

This goes totally against the idea of the wicked having some type of second chance to somehow recover or to get off the hook after death. It also rules out the concept of purgatory.

> 8 *The righteous is delivered out of the tribulation, and the wicked takes his place.*

During the prophesied and imminent great tribulation, the wicked will be removed from among the righteous. Many of those who invent escapist eschatology don't believe that it's possible for any of us to become truly righteous. They have ignored, twisted, or misunderstood what the Scripture states regarding perfection, righteousness, and uprightness.

From beginning to end, the Scripture contrasts the clean with the unclean, the righteous with the wicked, the just with the unjust, and so on. In God's eyes, there is no middle ground. At the time of the end, there will be those who are hot and those who are cold, but there is no room for the lukewarm (Revelation 3:16).

> 9 *The hypocrite with his mouth destroys his neighbor, but the just are delivered with wisdom.*

The hypocrite can do a lot of damage with his mouth. Jesus' message dealt with this throughout his ministry (Matthew 5, 6, 7, 23). He openly declared the religious leaders of his day to be hypocrites.

> 10 *When it goes well with the righteous,*
> *the city rejoices, and when the wicked per-*
> *ish, there are feasts.*

This reinforces the fact that the righteous will remain and the wicked will be removed from among them. This will be fulfilled at the last great feast, the Feast of Tabernacles. This is prophesied for the end of the harvest at the end of the age.

> 11 *By the blessing of the upright the city is*
> *exalted, but it is overthrown by the mouth*
> *of the wicked.*

Some cities will be exalted and others will be overthrown. The mouth of the wicked is sufficient to overthrow their cities. The blessing of the upright, on the other hand, comes from God, and no enemy can impede it.

> 12 *He that is void of understanding*
> *despises his neighbour, but the intelligent*
> *man remains silent.*

Only the Lord can change hearts. It is best for us to remain silent, therefore, unless and until the Lord moves us to speak. If we stir things up, our meddling may make it even harder for God to intervene.

> 13 *A talebearer reveals secrets, but he that*
> *is of a faithful spirit conceals the matter.*

There are many things that should not be revealed, even if they are true.

> 14 *When intelligence is lacking, the people shall fall, but in the multitude of counsellors there is salvation.*

True intelligence comes only from God. Those who have intelligence will bring salvation. We are called to be counselors, not controllers.

> 15 *With anxiety shall he that is surety for a stranger be afflicted, and he that hates suretiship shall live securely.*

A stranger is someone who doesn't know the Lord, and we should not vouch for them either in the material realm or in the spiritual realm.

> 16 *The gracious woman retains honour, and strong men retain riches.*

God desires for his people to retain our honor even if we lose worldly riches.

> 17 *The merciful man does good to his own soul, but the cruel man troubles his own flesh.*

The merciful person has a heart for others, which is vastly different from being surety for a stranger. The merciful will obtain mercy.

> 18 *The wicked works a deceitful work, but to him that sows righteousness shall be a sure reward.*

The wicked spend an enormous amount of time and energy doing things that will amount to nothing.

All the things and possessions of this world will come to nothing in the end. This is vastly different from the person who sows righteousness, and God assures us that ultimately such people will be rewarded.

> 19 *As righteousness is unto life, so he that pursues evil pursues it unto his own death.*

This is true in both the natural and the spiritual realms.

> 20 *They that are of a perverse heart are an abomination to the LORD, but such as are perfect in their way are his delight.*

The perverse heart excludes the presence of the Lord. Those who are perfect or mature in their way (in how they go about doing things) are his delight. Jesus is the way – the only way. It is only possible to be perfect in our way if we're being led and empowered by him, the source of all goodness.

> 21 *No matter how many covenants he has made with death, the wicked shall not be absolved, but the seed of the righteous shall escape.*

The seed of the righteous is singular. It includes all those who are in Christ. Those who continue to act wickedly will not be absolved, no matter how many "sinner's prayers" they've repeated or how many religious hoops they've jumped through. Only the seed of the righteous shall escape. In order to be righteous, we must be born again by the Spirit of God and come under the discipline and chastening of the heavenly Father. God wants to change our desires from the heart. No matter how many church services you attend or how many covenants you make, they will be of no avail unless the old man, with all of his wicked desires, dies. Just rehabilitating the old man isn't enough for God's purposes: he doesn't want us to be merely "in recovery," lest in our arrogance we continue seeking the things of this world. He wants us to start afresh as a new creation in him.

> 22 *As a gold ring in a swine's snout, so is a fair woman which is without discretion.*

This is true in the natural and also in the church.

> 23 *The desire of the righteous is only good, but the hope of the wicked is wrath.*

The righteous only desires good. This is another definition of perfection of the heart. The person who still has evil desires in his heart has not been converted. Conversion requires our will, but willpower isn't enough without the direct intervention and grace of God. If God doesn't do for us what we're unable to do for ourselves, our heart will not be perfect. His desire is to replace our old, stony heart with his soft, sensitive heart. When this happens, our appetites will change.

> 24 *There are those who scatter, and more is added unto them; and there are those who withhold more than is just, but come to poverty.*

Those who are generous will never lose.

> 25 *The soul who is a blessing unto others shall be made fat, and he that fills shall be filled also himself.*

Jesus said, *Blessed are those that hunger and thirst for righteousness for they shall be satisfied* (Matthew 5:6).

> 26 *He that withholds the grain, the people shall curse him, but blessing shall be upon the head of him that sells it.*

In times of famine or of siege, there would be hunger or even death if grain were to be hoarded. The story of Joseph in Egypt is very telling. He saved up grain during the seven years of good crops and then sold it during the seven years of famine.

The famine that is upon us now is a famine not of bread, but of hearing the words of the Lord (Amos 8:11). There are those who have been storing up grain, storing up the word of the Lord, and the time will soon come when we must begin to *sell*. In Joseph's time, the people used up all their money, sold all their animals, sold their land, and even sold themselves to Joseph to keep from starving to death. A spiritual version of this is about to take place in which the giving of tithes and offerings will not suffice. In order to survive the times, the private kingdoms and the carnal walks in the flesh must be surrendered and replaced with a total commitment to God.

Many think that things will continue as they are until the time of the "rapture," but they are very mistaken. Those who are carnal and lukewarm among the people of God think that the word and the spiritual gifts that they now have will continue to flow; but the current state of affairs will soon be interrupted and extinguished like the lamps of the foolish virgins (Matthew 25:8).

> 27 *He that seeks good early shall find*
> *favour, but unto him that seeks evil, it*
> *shall come upon him.*

Those who seek the things of this world are really seeking evil; for *whatsoever is not out of faith is sin* (Romans 14:23).

A human life will tend to go in one of two basic directions, seeking either good or evil. This will intensify as time goes on. Good continually gets better, and evil progressively becomes worse, with an ever-expanding gulf in between. The only way to seek good is to hearken unto the Lord. Those who seek evil have turned their back on the truth.

> 28 *He that trusts in his riches shall fall,*
> *but the righteous shall flourish as a*
> *branch.*

No amount of earthly wealth or riches will be enough to get us through what is coming upon the earth. Only real righteousness will suffice.

> 29 *He that troubles his own house shall*
> *inherit the wind, and the fool shall be*
> *slave to the wise of heart.*

The wise of heart will soon come out on top. Satan's house is divided. He must keep his own forces in line by troubling them with fear and terror, and thus he will lose the inheritance.

> 30 *The fruit of righteousness is a tree of*
> *life, and he that wins souls is wise.*

How do we win souls? With the fruit of righteousness:

the seed is in the fruit. The tree of life is related to the presence of God and to the healing of the nations. The tree of life grows in the midst of the plaza of the city of God and along the banks of the river of God, and it gives its fruit every month without fail (Revelation 22:2).

Those who are attempting to evangelize souls but do not demonstrate the fruit of righteousness in themselves are not wise. They have no incorruptible seed to plant.

> 31 *The righteous shall certainly be recompensed in the earth; how much more the wicked and the sinner!*

Each one will reap the fullness of what he has sown.

Proverbs 12

> 1 *Whosoever loves chastening loves knowledge, but he that hates reproof is carnal.*

Many teach that there are carnal Christians and spiritual Christians and we choose which of these we become.

Yes, it definitely is a choice, but carnal Christians may not be secure because they may not really be converted. Those who think they are secure as carnal Christians and God does not need to chasten them are fools, and in the coming tribulation they may or may not have time to rethink their position and cry out to God.

> 2 *The good man shall attain the favour of the LORD, but the man of wicked thoughts he will condemn.*

The carnal man is the man of sin; the carnal man

is the old man; the carnal man is at enmity with God. Thus, the carnal man must die if Christ is to live victorious in us.

> 3 *Man shall not be established by wickedness, but the root of the righteous shall not be moved.*

What is the root of the righteous? What is the root of the good olive tree? It is Christ, the root of all goodness and righteousness.

> 4 *The virtuous woman is a crown to her husband, but she that makes ashamed is as rottenness to his bones.*

Jesus will return for a perfect bride who will be a crown unto him. The witness of what God has done in and through her will give him the moral authority to judge and rule the world. In contrast, when Adam disobeyed God at the insistence of his deceived wife, they soon stood naked and ashamed before God. This caused him to lose the authority that God had given him.

The people of the Devil (we could think of them as the wife of the Devil) do not give him happiness. They do not overflow with love and affection; they reflect what the Devil has planted, which is strife and division.

Satan's kingdom is not secure. His people are going to make him ashamed; they are rottenness to his bones. The Devil's house is on shaky ground, and it will fall no matter how hard he attempts to prop it up. The wicked will soon be removed from among the righteous.

> 5 *The thoughts of the righteous are*

upright, but the astuteness of the wicked
is deceit.

The wicked deceive themselves and one another. The thoughts of the righteous are the mind of Christ.

6 *The words of the wicked are to lie in wait*
for blood, but the mouth of the upright
shall deliver them.

Even if they kill us for speaking the truth, God will include us in the first resurrection and cause us to reign and rule with Christ (Revelation 20:4).

7 *God shall overthrow the wicked, and*
they shall not be any longer, but the house
of the righteous shall remain.

Notice that all of these promises are conditional: that is, only those who belong to the house of the righteous will be saved. Notice that it does not say that those who sin in word, thought, or deed, or those who sin by omission shall remain; nor does it say that those who repeated a sinner's prayer or went forward at an evangelistic meeting shall remain. It says that the wicked shall be overthrown (no matter what religious activity they participated in) and that only the house of the righteous (righteousness and justice are the same word in Hebrew) shall remain. Only Jesus Christ is righteous, and he rules over his house; therefore, only those who allow him to rule over them will remain.

The houses of religion that are run by the strange woman teach that it is not possible for us to be just or righteous here on earth. They teach that we will inevitably continue to sin – whether in word, thought, deed, or by omission – on a daily basis and that the only way to absolve our guilt is by jumping through their religious hoops. They teach that there is no such thing as victory over personal sin, and they use the guilt from the defeat of their parishioners to stimulate them to come to confession or daily mass or pay their tithes or come to all worship services, prayer meetings, etc.

> 8 *A man shall be commended according to his wisdom, but he that is of a perverse heart shall be despised.*

If those who are perverse of heart talk too much, they will soon be found out and despised.

> 9 *He that despises himself and becomes a slave is better than he that honours himself and lacks bread.*

It is better to humble ourselves before the Lord with the attitude of a slave and let him lift us up in due time than to build ourselves up. If we rely on our own good opinion of ourselves, we will end up in a position of want. Remember the words of Romans 6:19-23: *I speak a human thing because of the weakness of our flesh: that as ye presented your members to serve uncleanness and iniquity unto iniquity, likewise now present your members to serve righteousness unto holiness. For being previously the slaves of sin, now ye have been made the slaves of righteousness. What fruit had ye then in those things of which ye are now ashamed? for the end of those things is death. But now freed from sin and made slaves to God, ye have as your fruit sanctification and as the*

*end, everlasting life. For the wages of sin is death, but
the grace of God is eternal life in Christ Jesus, our Lord.*

Jesus gave his life to redeem us. We were slaves to
sin, to the world, and to the Devil, but Jesus ransomed
us and set us free so we might serve God. Every slave
has an owner, and now we belong to God so we might
be slaves of righteousness. Righteousness is being what
God wants us to be in order to do his will.

> 10 *The righteous is merciful even unto his
> beast, but the piety of the wicked is cruel.*

When I'm walking around through the jungles and
mountains, I look for those who treat their animals
with mercy, because they will always make good guides.
Some, however, run around crying, "Glory to God!
Hallelujah!" but still mistreat their horses and mules.

> 11 *He that tills his land shall be satisfied
> with bread, but he that follows vain per-
> sons is void of understanding.*

We are made from the dust of the earth. In the
highest sense, we are the land that God desires to till.
If we allow the Lord to break up our fallow ground,
he will be able to cause us to bring forth the fruit of
righteousness. Some of those in pulpits all over the
world today are nothing more than *vain persons void
of understanding*, because they concentrate on success according to this world and do not submit to the
chastening of Father God. Multitudes follow them as
they go about piling up bundles of tares.

> 12 *The wicked desires the net of evil men,*

but the root of the righteous shall yield
fruit.

The nets of evil men, which snare men and women into religious or even political houses of ill repute, are in high demand for the wicked. Over history, the wicked have always laid nets and snares, and the righteous have always planted righteousness and produced good fruit by faith, by depending on God (Habakkuk 2:4; Romans 1:17).

> 13 *The wicked is snared by the transgression of his lips, but the just shall come out of the tribulation.*

The wicked are going to be snared and removed from among the righteous by the tribulation that is at the door (Revelation 2:22-23). The righteous shall come out of the tribulation purified and just. You'll notice that this does not say that the righteous will avoid the tribulation.

> 14 *Man shall be satisfied with good by the fruit of his mouth, and the recompense of a man's hands shall be rendered unto him.*

The good fruit of his mouth will satisfy the one who comes out of the tribulation pure and just. The only one who is good and righteous is Jesus Christ, and if we're satisfied with good by the fruit of our mouth, it's because God has perfected our heart. It is out of the fullness of the heart that the mouth speaks. Then the work of our hands will please God, and whatever we put our hand to will prosper.

15 *The way of the fool is right in his own
eyes, but he that hears counsel is wise.*

The fool will never seek counsel until it is too late.

16 *A fool's wrath is presently known, but
he who covers the injury is sane.*

A fool will lash out immediately if someone upsets
him.

17 *He that speaks truth shows forth righteousness, but a false witness, deceit.*

Now we are truthful witnesses of the grace and
power of God.

18 *There are those that speak like the
piercings of a sword, but the tongue of the
wise is medicine.*

This is why it's so important to choose our com-
panions well. If we take with us into delicate situations
someone who claims to know God and appears to be
a wonderful Christian, the situations may worsen if
these people use words as a weapon.

19 *The lip of truth shall be established
for ever, but a lying tongue is but for a
moment.*

Jesus is the truth and shall never be moved. Satan
is the father of lies and will soon be a fleeting memory.

20 *Deceit is in the heart of those whose
thoughts are evil, but joy in that of those
whose thoughts are good.*

It's impossible to cleanse the minds of those who

are evil; their hearts will never be happy, because they are full of deceit. Joy is the fruit of the Spirit, and it fills the hearts of those whose thoughts are good.

> 21 *No iniquity shall overtake the righteous; but the wicked shall be filled with evil.*

Iniquity is wrongdoing that the person is hiding from the light. No iniquity shall overtake the righteous because if God points out something that he doesn't like, they face it and deal with it by the grace (power) of God.

The righteous are protected and will not be overtaken by hidden sin.

> 22 *Lying lips are abomination to the LORD: but the workers of the truth are his delight.*

Lies and truth cannot flow from the same vessel. The Lord loves the workers of the truth. Lip service to the truth is not enough; we are to be workers of the truth. We are to be doers of the word, not just hearers (James 1:22).

> 23 *The sane man conceals his wisdom: but the heart of fools proclaims foolishness.*

Fools proclaim their foolishness. Those who are wise in the Lord know that they are really not wise of their own wisdom. They know the Lord is the one who is wise, and apart from him, they don't know anything. If the Lord doesn't give us the words to say, we must remain silent.

Those who are wise according to the Lord do not lead others to depend upon them; they lead others to depend directly upon the Lord. God does not give us wisdom to enable us to control or manipulate the lives of others; he gives it to help us lead others to make direct contact with him, so they can hear directly from him and be moved directly by him.

> 24 *The hand of the diligent shall bear rule:*
> *but the negligent shall be under tribute.*

Some are diligent; some are negligent. The diligent shall be the head, and the negligent shall be the tail. The diligent are those who hear the voice of God and do what he says. The negligent are those who know they should do good but fail to carry out that knowledge.

> 25 *Heaviness in the heart of man makes it*
> *stoop: but a good word makes it glad.*

God will encourage our hearts with a good word when we are diligent.

> 26 *The righteous causes his neighbor to*
> *consider: but the way of the wicked causes*
> *them to err.*

One way or another, we will have an effect on our neighbor.

> 27 *The deceitful man does not even roast*
> *that which he took in hunting: but the*
> *substance of a diligent man is precious.*

The diligent man feeds on what God provides. The intimate, private, personal word of the Lord is precious to him. The deceitful man takes prey that he doesn't even utilize. The Devil and his followers take prey and let it go to waste.

> 28 *In the way of righteousness is life; and*
> *in the pathway thereof there is no death.*

If you pass through the narrow gate and begin to be led by the Lord in the way of righteousness, your eternal destiny will change. You will begin to plant righteousness, and there will be an endless harvest of blessing unto eternal life. This pathway does not lead to death.

The way of righteousness leads to the tree of life. This is the life of God, which is not planted through plans and projects of men but may only be found by following the Spirit of God; but in order to have continual guidance from the Holy Spirit, we must submit to the correction and chastening of God the Father.

What does God desire?

If we turn around and seek him with all of our heart, he will lead us from where we are to where he wants us. If we put him first and seek his counsel regarding whatever responsibilities already exist in our lives, he will show us step by step how we are to manage everything. If we allow ourselves to be corrected when God shows us something that is wrong or that he does not like, he will place us on the path to maturity or perfection in Christ.

If we put the Lord first even in the little things, God will take care of the big things that are way beyond our ability to control. The most important things are matters of the heart. Before we know it, a chain reaction will begin that may have very far-reaching consequences for good. When the sons of God work righteousness by the power of the Spirit, the world will see the difference even as it relates to practical daily life (Matthew 5:16).

In the past God has used flawed human organizations, and he continues to use them today. God has worked and will work in spite of all the errors that men have committed in his name over the centuries. Now, however, is not the time for us to make more mistakes. This is the time to allow the Spirit of God to correct and to chasten us according to the desires of our heavenly Father, so we may come to individual and corporate repentance (Joel 1:13-14).

The Lord is doing something new that doesn't directly depend on human organizations. It depends on each person having a direct relationship with the Lord, so he can correct, chasten, and intervene whenever and however he desires. As he cleanses and purifies hearts, those who are pure and clean will be joined together by him, at his discretion, to form the bride of Christ – a glorious prospect!

Let Us Pray:

Heavenly Father, we ask that you may open our spiritual eyes so that we may see the huge difference when things are done your way. We ask that you may continue to prepare the bride of Christ so that for the first time in history, your people may be put on display as a clean woman, a clean corporate manifestation of your love and goodness upon the earth. We ask this in the name of our Lord Jesus Christ. Amen.

Meet the Author

Russell Stendal, a former hostage of Colombian rebels, is a lifelong missionary to that same group in the jungles of Colombia. He is an influential friend to military and government leaders in Colombia, Cuba, Mexico, Venezuela, and the United States. Russell's ministry shares the gospel via twelve radio stations, hundreds of thousands of Bibles, books, and movies distributed through airplane parachute drops, and numerous speaking engagements for groups of leaders, prisoners, and individuals. Russell goes wherever the Lord leads, whether it's to speak with a president or to go deep into the jungle to help an individual in trouble. He has witnessed thousands commit their lives to Christ.

Connect with the Author

Website: www.cpcsociety.ca
Newsletter Signup:www.anekopress.com/
stendal-newsletter

Russell and his coworkers have built dozens of radio stations in Latin America that concentrate a clear message on remote and dangerous areas where persecution of Christians is rampant. More than 120,000 Galcom solar-powered radios have been deployed to those being discipled. Most of the programming is in Spanish, but they also transmit in almost a dozen native languages where a great move of God  is presently taking place. Russell preaches through the Bible, a chapter or so per message. More than 1,000 messages have been recorded and aired repeatedly. The chapters of this book are samples of these messages preached on the radio in the Colombian war zone about ten years ago. The key website is www.fuerzadepaz.com. Pray for Russell and his team as they expand Spanish-language radio coverage into places like Cuba, Venezuela, Mexico, and Central America.

Plans are in the works for new stations broadcasting in English that will provide coverage into Africa (where there are over 300 million English speakers) and possibly even into Asia and the Middle East. The first stage, as the programming is refined, will be Internet radio. After that, we want to begin shortwave radio transmission and distribution of Galcom radios in Africa and elsewhere as God opens the doors. The new radios have digital audio Bibles on board, and the goal is to move in the direction of digital shortwave transmissions within the next few years.

Connect with Russell's Ministry

Website

www.cpcsociety.ca

Receive newsletter updates

http://goo.gl/amBsCD

Buy books

http://amzn.to/1nPLcNL

jubilee
B I B L E 2000

*Hear what God is
saying through this
original translation*

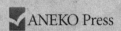

ANEKO Press

Made in the USA
Columbia, SC
26 August 2017